A Three-Fold Cord

*God Bears Witness to His Salvation
Plan for Mankind: The Death, Burial
and Resurrection of Jesus Christ*

Phillip Stuckemeyer

authorHOUSE®

AuthorHouse™
1663 Liberty Drive
Bloomington, IN 47403
www.authorhouse.com
Phone: 1-800-839-8640

Contact the author with comments or inquiries
at the following e-mail address:
phil@stuckemeyer.com

© 2011 Phillip Stuckemeyer. All rights reserved.

No part of this book may be reproduced, stored in
a retrieval system, or transmitted by any means
without the written permission of the author.

First published by AuthorHouse 3/15/2011

ISBN: 978-1-4567-2796-3 (sc)
ISBN: 978-1-4567-2795-6 (e)

Library of Congress Control Number: 2011901562

Printed in the United States of America

Any people depicted in stock imagery provided by Thinkstock are models,
and such images are being used for illustrative purposes only.
Certain stock imagery © Thinkstock.

This book is printed on acid-free paper.

Because of the dynamic nature of the Internet, any web addresses or
links contained in this book may have changed since publication and
may no longer be valid. The views expressed in this work are solely those
of the author and do not necessarily reflect the views of the publisher,
and the publisher hereby disclaims any responsibility for them.

Table of Contents

Why this book, and why now?	vii
A Three-Fold Cord – What does it mean?	ix
<u>Section 1 – The Ancient Types</u>	1
Chapter 1 – The Big Picture	3
Chapter 2 – God's Promise to Adam & Eve	8
Chapter 3 – A Promise to Abraham and Isaac	10
Chapter 4 – The Exodus	16
Chapter 5 – A Divine Pattern in the Heavenlies	29
Chapter 6 – The Tabernacle of Moses	34
Chapter 7 – The Only Way to God	40
Chapter 8 – The Sign of the Prophet Jonah	55
Chapter 9 – A Voice Crying in the Wilderness	58
<u>Section 2 – Messiah's Fulfillment</u>	61
Chapter 10 – The Life of Jesus	63
Chapter 11 – The Witness of God	71
Chapter 12 – Poured Out at Calvary	74
Chapter 13 – The Passion of Christ	76
<u>Section 3 – A Timeless Salvation</u>	84
Chapter 14 – Past, Present and Future	89
Chapter 15 – The Great Commission	92
<u>Section 4 – Future Grace</u>	100
Chapter 16 – The Keys to the Kingdom	115
Chapter 17 – It Is Written	120
Chapter 18 – It Behooved Christ	125
Chapter 19 – Preach In His Name	128
Chapter 20 – The Testimony of Peter	136

Chapter 21 – The Testimony of Philip	141
Chapter 22 – Peter Defends His Testimony	146
Chapter 23 – The Testimony of Paul	153
Chapter 24 – The Essence of the Gospel	163
Chapter 25 – Conclusion	169

Why this book, and why now?

Joshua 24:15 And if it seem evil unto you to serve the LORD, <u>choose you this day whom ye will serve</u>... but as for me and my house, we will serve the LORD.

2 Peter 1:10 Wherefore the rather, brethren, <u>give diligence to make your calling and election sure</u>...

11 For so an entrance shall be ministered unto you abundantly into the everlasting kingdom of our Lord and Saviour...

12 Wherefore I will not be negligent to put you always in remembrance of these things, though ye know them, and be established in the present truth.

The Gospel of Jesus Christ must be proclaimed in all the earth before the end; however, the end will come sooner for some than for others. Each of us decides what and in whom we believe, and that decision has a profound impact on destiny. Whether or not you buy this opening paragraph may very well determine if you continue to read the rest of the book. I pray that you do.

This book is for believers and unbelievers alike. Those who do not trust in Jesus Christ will be skeptical at first, and I hope to offer them a fresh look at an old story that has been poorly told on many occasions. And even you who do believe in Jesus can benefit from this book. Please allow me to confirm and strengthen your life in Christ, but also to challenge myths that may weaken your faith.

A new day is dawning, and it is time for everyone to decide whom they will serve. I encourage you to allow the Bible to say what God intends for it to say, and to realize that it means only what God intends for it to mean. If anyone tries to make the scripture mean something other than what the great King meant to say when the words were penned, servants of the Lord are duty bound to resist and expose such lies. Soldiers in the army of the Lord must be vigilant. There is an adversary, and he will stop at nothing to steal, kill and ultimately destroy the weak and defenseless.

The battle is raging, and it is high time to serve the Lord. Allegiance to Jesus requires obedience to his word. Christians everywhere should take a new look at the old book. I hope that you will honestly assess what you believe, and make sure that your trust is only in the Jesus of the Bible.

I pray that this book strengthens the people of God and furthers the cause of the Gospel. There is nothing novel or innovative about the Gospel. The Present Truth has always been and will always be the only truth. The Gospel of Jesus Christ has always been and will always be the only way of salvation.

A Three-Fold Cord

What does it mean?

Psalm 11:3 If the foundations be destroyed, what can the righteous do?

The Holy Bible makes several dramatic declarations that seem to have been completely overlooked by a great number of Bible scholars and ministers. When was the last time that you heard a Bible preacher or teacher make a statement like:

"I declare unto you the gospel"

I imagine it may have been within the last few weeks that someone announced they were going to tell you how you can be saved. It may have been on the job, on a street corner, on a television show, or in a church. There are millions of voices telling us how to be saved, many of them offering a hope based upon the life of a historic figure known as Jesus Christ. This hope often rests on a variety of faulty assumptions. Typically, we are told we should:

- o   be a good person.
- o   join a certain church.
- o   do certain things, and don't do other things.

- o   be really, really sincere.
- o   just believe.

When any conversation turns toward the basic human desire for life after death, opinions abound. These opinions contain many lovely sentiments, but whose opinion is correct? And whose opinion really matters anyhow? Here is a news flash!

My opinion doesn't matter!

Your opinion doesn't matter either!

Only God's opinion matters!

Let me be perfectly clear. God doesn't really have opinions! God simply knows the truth about everything. In fact, God is the sole arbiter, or judge of truth. God invented truth. God is truth.

John 14:6 Jesus saith unto him, I am the way, the truth, and the life: no man cometh unto the Father, but by me.

God's opinions (truths) have been expressed in his own words, and recorded as Holy Scripture. The scriptures contain the good news, or the Gospel message that we can be saved from the terrible ravages of sin, escaping its penalty of death and damnation. Here is what the Bible says:

1 Corinthians 15:1 Moreover, brethren, I declare unto you the gospel which I preached unto you, which also ye have received, and wherein ye stand;

2 By which also ye are saved, if ye keep in memory what I preached unto you, unless ye have believed in vain.

3 For I delivered unto you first of all that which I also received, how that Christ died for our sins according to the scriptures;

4 And that he was buried, and that he rose again the third day according to the scriptures:

5 And that he was seen of Cephas, then of the twelve:

6 After that, he was seen of above five hundred brethren at once; of whom the greater part remain unto this present, but some are fallen asleep.

7 After that, he was seen of James; then of all the apostles.

8 And last of all he was seen of me also, as of one born out of due time.

These words were penned by a messenger from God named Paul, and here in a nutshell is what he said:

1. I'm going to explain the Gospel.
2. This is what I preach.
3. This is the basis for your salvation.
4. Don't forget these things.
5. **Jesus died**, just like the Bible said he would.
6. **Jesus was buried**, as the Bible promised.
7. **Jesus arose from the dead**, as was predicted.
8. There are many witnesses who saw Jesus after he arose from the dead, specifically:
    a. Peter
    b. The twelve disciples as a group

c. Another group of over 500 brethren
   d. A person named James
   e. The apostles, sent to spread the news
   f. Paul himself, on a trip to Damascus.

There it is! **This is the Gospel of Jesus Christ.**

What is Paul really saying? There are three essential elements to the Gospel message. Jesus Christ died for our sins, was laid to rest in the grave, but arose from the dead. Furthermore, Paul insists that these happenings were completely consistent with the Holy Scriptures, and can be verified by a careful examination of the eye witness testimony. Paul felt so strongly about this Gospel, he was actually willing to go on record with an explicit claim that your salvation depends on the truth of this simple message. Believe it or scoff at it, but the Gospel is:

The Death, Burial, and Resurrection of the Messiah.

This is "**The Three-Fold Cord**" of prophetic history!

The premise of this book is that the most basic, foundational truths of the Gospel message have largely been missed by the bulk of Christian ministers. Actually, the subtext behind the premise is that there is an ongoing conspiracy to suppress and subvert the salvation message. There are enemies of the human race who work tirelessly to so baffle and confuse the many sincere and well-meaning members of the clergy that the righteous people of God must wade through a mountain of ideological garbage on their way to the city of God. These enemies of the Cross exert powerful influences on an institutional system of

Seminaries, Bible Schools, and Denominational hierarchies in a most blatant attempt to hoodwink the masses into an early grave and an eternal hell.

As the Psalmist wrote, when the foundation of any structure is hopelessly flawed, what can be done to restore it? Sometimes you just have to dig it all up and start over. This book is a call to action for all committed believers in Jesus Christ to take another look at the Gospel message. Our great mission and our fervent hope is that the Gospel will triumph, as an old prophet said:

Habakkuk 2:14 For the earth shall be filled with the knowledge of the glory of the LORD, as the waters cover the sea.

But upon what is this blessed hope founded? It rests on nothing less than the truth of God's word. Any message that is not consistent with the Gospel of the Bible is not The Gospel.

As song writer Edward Mote wrote in 1832:

> On Christ the solid rock I stand
> All other ground is sinking sand
> All other ground is sinking sand

I am convinced that God has been engaged in a six thousand year campaign to save sinners and that all across this period of time the same simple message of hope and deliverance has been proclaimed by official emissaries sent forth from his throne.

I must add that this message has been faithfully delivered to the human race in a fashion that is so consistent and so complete that its veracity cannot be denied by any person who honestly considers its basic claims.

A Three-Fold Cord is not just the title of this book. God has, from the beginning of time, woven the thread of truth throughout all his dealings with mankind. This three-fold message has been purposefully and progressively revealed throughout the whole of Judeo-Christian literature and experience. The one, true and sovereign God has chosen to systematically reveal his plan to salvage a remnant, and this revelation cannot be understood apart from his own authoritative testimony. Listen to the Word of God as he bears witness to this truth:

1 John 5:8 And there are three that bear witness in earth, the Spirit, and the water, and the blood: and these three agree in one.

9 If we receive the witness of men, the witness of God is greater: for this is the witness of God which he hath testified of his Son.

You may have heard that there is a Scarlet Thread that runs through the Bible. I have further developed that idea, and will show that there is actually a Three-Fold Cord woven throughout the scriptures, from Genesis to Revelation. This consistent theme is God's testimony about the marvelous plan of salvation that he has so graciously provided for us from the beginning.

Blood	Water	Spirit
Death	Burial	Resurrection
Repentance	Baptism	Holy Spirit

This is the witness of God!

Ecclesiastes 4:12 And if one prevail against him, two shall withstand him; and a threefold cord is not quickly broken.

You may be tempted to look elsewhere for your inspiration. I did a quick search of the internet and found plenty of other applications of the three-fold cord. Here are a few examples:

Peace	Hope	Love
You	Me	God
Husband	Wife	Children
Father	Son	Holy Spirit

In most cases the message seems to be that there is strength in numbers, or that we should be united in a common purpose.

A literal interpretation of Ecclesiastes 4:12 is really quite useful. Winding three smaller cords together to make one larger rope increases its strength exponentially. This truth has benefitted multiplied millions of people who were trying to move heavy objects or were building large structures.

The book of Ecclesiastes was written nearly 1000 years before the ministry of Jesus Christ, and long after the development of rope:

- o Egyptian rope dates back to 4000 to 3500 B.C. and was generally made of water reed fibres.
- o Starting from approximately 2800 B.C., rope made of hemp fibres was in use in China.
- o Twisted ropes are built up in three steps. First, fibres are gathered and spun to form yarns. A number of these yarns are then twisted together to form strands. The strands are then twisted together to form the rope. The twist of the yarn is opposite to that of the strand, and that in turn is opposite to that of the rope. It is this counter-twist, introduced with each successive operation, which holds the final rope together as a stable, unified object.

The Bible agrees that a triple-stranded rope is worth every penny you will pay for it. But is there a deeper meaning to Ecclesiastes 4:12? Yes! God has a profound spiritual application in mind.

Excellent Things

Proverbs 22:20 Have not I written to thee excellent things in counsels and knowledge,

21 That I might make thee know the certainty of the words of truth; that thou mightest answer the words of truth to them that send unto thee?

Young's Literal Translation of the Bible gives us additional insight into the meaning of Excellent:

Proverbs 22:20 Have I not written to thee three times with counsels and knowledge?

Strong's Exhaustive Concordance adds this clarification:

> "Excellent: a triple, a three-fold measure, as a musical instrument with three strings."

God wants us to know the truth, and he often emphasizes critically important points through repetition. Because the same message is declared again and again, the people of God are better able to be certain of the important details. The truth is established by the testimony of multiple witnesses. This principle has been declared in both the Old Testament and the New Testament.

Deuteronomy 17:6 At the mouth of two witnesses, or three witnesses, shall he that is worthy of death be put to death; but at the mouth of one witness he shall not be put to death.

2 Corinthians 13:1 This is the third time I am coming to you. In the mouth of two or three witnesses shall every word be established.

The significance of Three-Fold things goes far beyond the implications of simple repetition. Theologians consider the number 3 to be the number of divine perfection. The thought, then, is that Three-Fold things are not just Excellent things, but that they are solid, real, substantial, complete, and entire. Three-Fold things are Perfect things.

God has revealed his truth in a Three-Fold fashion, and this book explores that very premise. The Three-Fold Cord that is woven throughout the entire Bible is the witness of God, testifying to the salvation that is made available to us through the Death, Burial, and Resurrection of Jesus Christ. The witness of God is reliable and trustworthy. The witness of God does not lack for sufficient detail or clarity. The witness of God is unimpeachable!

1 John 5:8 And there are three that bear witness in earth, the Spirit, and the water, and the blood: and these three agree in one.

9 If we receive the witness of men, the witness of God is greater: for this is the witness of God which he hath testified of his Son.

If you are searching for the truth, you can do no better than to take heed to the witness of God.

Section 1

The Ancient Types

Isaiah 45:21 ...<u>who hath declared this from ancient time</u>? who hath told it from that time? have not I the LORD? and there is no God else beside me; a just God and a Saviour; there is none beside me.

Isaiah 46:9 <u>Remember the former things of old</u>: for I am God, and there is none else...

10 Declaring the end from the beginning, and from ancient times the things that are not yet done, saying, <u>My counsel shall stand, and I will do all my pleasure</u>:

The Old Testament is full of types and shadows that help us understand New Testament truth.

Typology is the study of these types and shadows. The Merriam-Webster Dictionary offers a definition:

>TYPOLOGY
>
>1: a doctrine of theological types; especially: one

> holding that things in Christian belief are prefigured or symbolized by things in the Old Testament
>
> 2: study of or analysis or classification based on types or categories

The first nine chapters of this book are focused on what the Old Testament has to tell us about the salvation that God will send through the promised Messiah. Admittedly, there are many other types and shadows that we do not have time to consider.

Chapter 1

The Big Picture

God is Omnipotent, Omnipresent, Omniscient, and Eternal. These are technical words that simply mean God can do anything, he is everywhere, he knows everything, and he is ageless, spanning time and space. In fact, God existed before time or space existed, and he will continue without end even after it is declared that "there should be time no longer" (see Isaiah 60:20 and Revelation 10:6). Not only is God completely unshackled by the limitations of the time-space continuum, the Bible declares that he knows the end from the beginning. God has a plan to salvage the human race from the merciless ravages of sin, and he has openly declared this plan from day one. Isaiah, in chapters 45 and 46, clearly states that God, who is a Saviour, has been telling the details of this plan from the very start. From ancient times this salvation has been revealed.

There have always been counterfeit gods and fake religious alternatives to Yahweh's sovereign will; but make no mistake about one thing. There is no other God. There is no other Saviour. There is no other plan of salvation. There is no other hope. There is no other path that leads to eternal life. The all knowing, all powerful Creator of all things has declared what he will do, and he will surely do it! This progressive revelation was repeatedly foretold by the prophets.

Isaiah 28:13 But the word of the LORD was unto them precept upon precept, precept upon precept; line upon line, line upon line; here a little, and there a little; that they might go, and fall backward, and be broken, and snared, and taken.

This statement takes my breath away! Is it possible that God's purpose is NOT the salvation of every man, woman and child? Is it true that God's holiness and justice demand that sinners face the morbid consequences of their actions? Yes. This is true. The salvation plan of which I am writing has been shrouded in mystery for thousands of years. Yet, it is also true that a remnant has been granted glimpses of these mysterious truths from time to time, and it is the mighty God who determines when, how, and to whom each piece of the puzzle is revealed.

The reasons for which God has chosen a few persons here and there has little to do with the character of those persons, and everything to do with the character of God who is not only holy and just, but also merciful and kind. The heroes of the Bible were not chosen because God saw some special measure of godliness in them. God chose his messengers from among a talent pool of sinners who can rightly be described as wicked and doomed. The biblical narrative does not mince words in this regard. As we read the stories in the Bible we are consistently presented with the flaws and foibles, the sins and open rebellion of such miscreants as the adulterer and murderer David, the liar and trickster Jacob, and the weak and vulgar Peter. Yet God transforms those he chooses into mighty overcomers, and this transformation is possible because of the grace of a God who has the sovereign right to make such choices as he sees fit.

1 Peter 1:3 Blessed be the God and Father of our Lord Jesus Christ, which according to his abundant mercy hath begotten us again unto a lively hope by the resurrection of Jesus Christ from the dead,

4 To an inheritance incorruptible, and undefiled, and that fadeth not away, reserved in heaven for you,

5 Who are kept by the power of God through faith unto salvation ready to be revealed in the last time.

The reasons for which God has chosen to reveal pieces and parts of his salvation plan to a select group of people include one obvious purpose: the writing of the Holy Scripture. God did not endow a few authors with the revelation of the ages so that they could have the next big hit on the Amazon or New York Times lists of best selling books, nor was it so that the basis for the next apocalyptic blockbuster movie could be put to paper. No, the purpose of God is focused on the forming of a people at the end of an age. The church of Jesus Christ is the people. The time is now!

A look at the big picture is a look from the vantage point of a God who sees all and knows all. It is not possible for us to see, from our limited perspective, what God sees from his Throne on high. He sees it all, while we only see a little part. He sees the end and the beginning at the same time, while we can barely understand what is happening in our lives today. Though God has chosen to reveal the big picture in the pages of the scripture, not all who were bought by the blood of the Lamb have the advantage of hindsight. While Abraham and Isaac looked forward to the Cross, we can look back through the annals of time and see history in the light of the Cross. We would do well to seize this opportunity.

I would like to finish this chapter by asking each reader to carefully consider the biblical record of human history. What action has God taken directly that affects every human being? In what ways has God chosen to intervene in the historical narrative of the entire human race on a global scale? This is the big picture:

1. God gave life to every human. (Genesis 2:7)
2. God's judgment of sin drove every man, woman and child into a state of separation called "death." (Romans 5:12)
3. God purged the earth of the filth of sin, burying everything in a watery grave known as the flood. (Genesis 6:17)
4. God saved the human race by that same great flood: out of the water came forth hope for a new life. (1 Peter 3:20)
5. God shed his blood for the sins of the world. (1 John 2:2)
6. God poured out his Spirit of life and peace upon the entire human population. (Joel 2:28 and Acts 2:17)
7. God will shortly judge all men, holding them accountable for misdeeds and missed opportunities. (Hebrews 9:26-28)

God's solution for sin involves blood, water and spirit. Death, burial and resurrection are constantly recurring themes. I have set out to prove that every presentation of the Gospel in the Bible will be true to the same God breathed set of foundational principles.

Chapter 2

God's Promise to Adam & Eve

Genesis 3:15 And <u>I will put enmity</u> between thee and the woman, and <u>between thy seed and her seed</u>; it shall bruise thy head, and <u>thou shalt bruise his heel</u>.

The unthinkable had happened. All that the Creator had asked was that they enjoy life, dress the garden, bear children, and trust that he knew what was best for them. He provided everything that they would ever need. Their home was truly a paradise, designed specifically for them. Food, climate controls, companionship, meaningful activity, and regular fellowship with the object of their love and devotion: the Lord God himself. Yet, the tempter asked a provocative question: Hath God said? He asked the woman who, according to the biblical record, had not been present when God gave the commandment.

Was it possible that life would be more full and satisfying if she and the man could be like God? She ate, and gave the fruit to the man. Adam had the authority to put an end to the madness, but he chose the woman, rather than trusting in God. All he had to do was believe that God knew what was best. Like many modern men, however, he compromised his principles, opting for domestic peace and tranquility rather than obedience. Suddenly they knew evil, and they ran and hid in fear of death.

God had always known that the man would respond in unbelief, and God had a plan. He had a solution for the problem of sin and death. That solution was... death! The innocent must die, in order that the guilty might go free. The immediate problem is that Adam and Eve are ashamed of their nakedness. Death was unknown in the Garden, and it is likely that Adam and Eve watched in horror as the animal skins were taken for clothing. What an object lesson! Unbelief leads to sin. Sin brings shame, fear, bondage and death.

God's long term solution for sin is embodied in a promise. A son will be born. A miracle child will save the world. The enemy will attack, but the son will triumph. The man-child will be wounded in the battle, but the serpent's head will be mortally crushed.

Every generation longs for the birth of the promised son. Many sons are born to disappointed and desperate parents. The promise is repeated from generation to generation, while the doomed can only await its fulfillment.

As time goes by, the promise will be restated again and again. The prophets will clarify its rather ambiguous language. The Seed of the Woman? Yes! A virgin will conceive, and bring forth a son. (See Isaiah 7:14) God is faithful to keep his promise!

Chapter 3

A Promise to Abraham and Isaac

Genesis 12:3 And I will bless them that bless thee, and curse him that curseth thee: <u>and in thee shall all families of the earth be blessed</u>.

Hebrews 11:11 Through faith also <u>Sara herself received strength to conceive seed, and was delivered of a child when she was past age</u>, because she judged him faithful who had promised.

12 Therefore sprang there even of one, and him as good as dead, so many as the stars of the sky in multitude...

Many generations have passed. The world has been destroyed by a great flood. The languages have been confused at the tower of Babel, stifling the progress of those who opposed the will of God. The world's families have begun to migrate around the globe. Faith in God has waned, and many pagan religions have pushed the promise of God's Saviour out of the minds of the world's nations. Yet, God has a plan. In fact, God's plan is right on schedule. The promise of God is sure.

In order to bring forth this promised salvation, God will isolate a family, separate a nation, and preserve a righteous bloodline. The drama begins with a man named Abram, and his wife Sarai. Abram answers the call of God, departing from his pagan roots and following where the Lord leads. God's plan is now focused on a man and a woman, walking the land, laying claim to the promises of property, posterity, blessing, and salvation. The Bible says:

Hebrews 11:10 For he looked for a city which hath foundations, whose builder and maker is God.

From such humble beginnings a master plan begins to unfold. The theme that will be found throughout the remainder of the history of mankind will now prominently feature:

- o A man and a woman,
- o walking the land,
- o trusting in God's promise,
- o bringing forth a man-child, and
- o saving the world.

The pattern is to be repeated again and again as Isaac and Rebekeh, Boaz and Ruth, Joseph and Mary, and ultimately Jesus and his Bride fulfill the promise, bringing forth the desire of all nations.

Notice what God had said to Abram:

Genesis 12:2 And I will make of thee a great nation...

Implicit in this part of the promise is that Abram and Sarai will have children, and that from this union a great nation will arise.

Genesis 12:3 ...and in thee shall all families of the earth be blessed.

Not only will there be a people, but from this bloodline will come forth the Saviour of the world! The same promise that was made to Adam and Eve has now been extended to Abram and Sarai. But the story takes an unexpected turn. The promise of God is not to be fulfilled by the strength and vitality of men or women. Only the power of God can bring forth the miracle child, and Abraham and Sarah have not been allowed to see all the details in advance. They must live and serve by faith.

The years go by, and Sarah is barren. Perplexed, they look for an alternative means by which God might keep his promise. It's not that they doubted the veracity of God's promise, but they feared that they were mistaken about what he really meant.

When both the man and the woman were well past child rearing age, God kept his promise in a miraculous way. In effect, Sarah's womb was restored to vitality, and the promised son was born. Isaac was the joy of both Abraham and Sarah.

Genesis 21:1 And the LORD visited Sarah...

A Three-Fold Cord

2 For Sarah conceived, and bare Abraham a son in his old age...

5 And Abraham was an hundred years old, when his son Isaac was born unto him.

At last they had an heir who would not only inherit the property, but who would also inherit the promise of a Saviour. They never would have guessed what God was about to do, as the stage was set for the unfolding of one of the most amazing prophetic dramas in recorded history.

The story is told in Genesis 22. The prophetic nature of the language in the Scripture cannot be mistaken.

Genesis 22:2 Take now thy son, thine only son Isaac...

Thousands of years later, a Father would voluntarily give his Son to be the sin bearer whose life is sacrificed so that you and I might be saved. This dramatic presentation is a mere shadow of things to come in the future. "Thine only son" speaks of Jesus!

The prophetic saga continues. After what was probably a night of pure anguish, Abraham obediently takes his only son and leaves for the mountain of God. Their destination is not just any mountain, but is quite likely the very mountain upon which the Lord Jesus Christ is to be crucified. The journey takes three days, thus commemorating the three days and three nights that Jesus would lie in the grave. As Abraham stretched forth his hand to slay his willing victim (I say willing because there is simply no way that a man who was more than 100 years old could have forced the lad to hold still while he bound him with ropes.) the angel intervened. As Abraham had assured his son:

Genesis 22:8 God will provide himself a lamb...

The boy had asked, and his father had answered. Abraham had wrestled with the apparent contradiction for days. How is it possible that God, who had promised an unbroken line to the Saviour, could demand the death of Isaac? The answer? If a death is necessary, then a resurrection is equally as necessary.

Hebrews 11:17 By faith Abraham, when he was tried, offered up Isaac: and he that had received the promises offered up his only begotten son,

18 Of whom it was said, That in Isaac shall thy seed be called:

19 Counting that God was able to raise him up, even from the dead; from whence also he received him in a figure.

The story of Abraham and Isaac is an early prophetic representation of the Gospel message.

1. The promised, miracle child must die.
2. He will lie in the tomb for a full three days and nights.
3. On the third day he will arise from the dead.

Without realizing the meaning of these events, Abraham exercised faith in an early manifestation of the plan of

God to save sinners through the Death, Burial, and Resurrection of the Son of God.

What a revelation! What a perfect picture of the future! Abraham believed God, and it was counted as righteousness. (Genesis 15:6)

The same promise will be repeated to Isaac once he reaches adulthood (Genesis 26:2-4) and again to his son Jacob. (Genesis 28:13, 14)

Abraham, Isaac and Jacob were all flawed and imperfect men, as were all those who followed after them. Sin renders mortal men completely unworthy of the saving grace of God. The sin problem cannot be ignored. God has a plan!

Chapter 4

The Exodus

Exodus 12:5 <u>Your lamb shall be without blemish</u>, a male of the first year: ye shall take it out from the sheep, or from the goats:

6 ...<u>kill it</u> in the evening.

7 ...<u>take of the blood, and strike it on the two side posts and on the upper door post of the houses</u>...

Exodus 14:27 ...<u>the LORD overthrew the Egyptians in the midst of the sea</u>.

28 ...there remained not so much as one of them.

29 But the children of Israel walked upon dry land...

30 Thus the LORD saved Israel that day...

Joshua 3:14 ...when the people removed... to pass over Jordan

15 <u>And as... the feet of the priests that bare the ark were dipped in the brim of the water</u>...

16 ...<u>the waters... were cut off</u>: and the people passed over right against Jericho.

A Three-Fold Cord

The children of Israel have been enslaved by an Egyptian King. Egypt represents the bondage of sin, but God has a plan to liberate his people in what will prove to be a story of truly epic proportions. Moses is recalled to active duty from the backside of the desert, and his message consists of a simple demand: Let my people go! Pharaoh refuses. The contest begins!

A series of ten plagues shows forth the absolute supremacy of the one true God of Israel over the many false gods of Egypt. All the land of Egypt suffers through the first three plagues, even the descendants of Abraham. Pharaoh's magicians are able to duplicate only the first two plagues, and then they surrender to a power that they could only call "the finger of God." (Exodus 8:18, 19)

The children of Israel are exempted from the six plagues that follow, making it clear that the Lord's favor is upon his people. He has heard their cries for help, and has come to deliver them. But if God loves his chosen nation, why did he allow them to go into Egypt in the first place? The answer is a stunning declaration of the sovereignty of a Holy God determined to save a sinful people. God had revealed it to Abraham long ago.

Genesis 15:13 And he said unto Abram, Know of a surety that thy seed shall be a stranger in a land that is not theirs, and shall serve them; and they shall afflict them four hundred years;

14 And also that nation, whom they shall serve, will I judge: and afterward shall they come out with great substance.

God's people had fled to Egypt to escape famine, and grew content until they were forced into bondage by a hostile regime. If they had remained in the land of promise and trusted in the God of the promise, this might never have happened. Unbelief is the root cause of all heartache and sorrow. If we would simply believe what God has said, we could live the abundant life free of fear and its awful consequences.

The God who knows all and sees all has prepared in advance to show forth his mighty power in the liberating of his people. In the process God will also bear witness to his salvation plan.

The tenth judgment upon Egypt is the death of the firstborn. The death sentence is pronounced upon all families and households. The only chance to escape the Death Angel involves a transfer of the penalty upon the innocent Lamb of God.

Exodus 12:3 Speak ye unto all the congregation of Israel, saying, In the tenth day of this month they shall take to them every man a lamb, according to the house of their fathers, a lamb for an house:

4 And if the household be too little for the lamb, let him and his neighbour next unto his house take it according to the number of the souls; every man according to his eating shall make your count for the lamb.

5 Your lamb shall be without blemish, a male of the first year: ye shall take it out from the sheep, or from the goats:

The lamb that is to be sacrificed must be without blemish, perfect. This sacrificial lamb prefigures the Lord Jesus Christ. His blood, once it has been shed, must be applied to the dwelling place. When God sees the blood of the Lamb, he passes over the sinner. It is enough. His wrath is abated.

Exodus 12:6 And ye shall keep it up until the fourteenth day of the same month: and the whole assembly of the congregation of Israel shall kill it in the evening.

7 And they shall take of the blood, and strike it on the two side posts and on the upper door post of the houses, wherein they shall eat it.

Here we see those who are in bondage taking the blood of the lamb and applying it to the dwelling place. If you can imagine taking a paint brush that is dripping with red paint and splashing it against the top of your front door frame, and then splashing it against the right and left sides of the same door frame, you should also be able to imagine the shape of a cross that is suggested by this action. It is intriguing that God would require such a thing of his people. Do they understand? Probably not. Do they need to understand? Definitely not! What really matters is a reliance on the promise of a faithful God. By obedience they are exercising faith in an early demonstration of the plan and purpose of God to deliver his people from the bondage of sin through the shedding of innocent blood. Yes, it is figurative. Yes, it is symbolic. Yes, it is forward looking. But, it is nothing less than trust in the Lord Jesus Christ that saves them. That was God's plan then; and it is God's plan now. Do you object? How can you possibly suppose that the blood of the Lamb did not have power to save in the olden days?

Revelation 13:8 And all that dwell upon the earth shall worship him, whose names are not written in the book of life of the Lamb slain from the foundation of the world.

9 If any man have an ear, let him hear.

The Lamb was slain before the foundation of the world! It was a done deal even in that day. God's power and authority are not limited by time. Hear the word of the Lord!

The morning after Passover is greeted by sounds of weeping and cries of anguish as the Egyptians find their firstborn dead. But in the homes of Israel there is rejoicing. Surrounded by the evidence that sin kills and faith saves, they are still captives in a foreign land. It is time to follow the Lord out of Egypt!

Even today, when a sinner places his trust in the blood of the Lamb, he is immediately exempted from the penalty of sin. However, he is still encircled by the tangible circumstances that attend a life on planet earth with all its sin and degradation. The new believer in Jesus still must report to his job, and interact with his coworkers. His family members do not understand that everything is different now. The world expects that everything should remain the same. Did you lie, cheat and steal before Christ? Your friends will demand that you remain in your sin. They will accept no other behavior, and peer pressure is a terrible and powerful force.

Exodus 13:21 And the LORD went before them by day in a pillar of a cloud, to lead them the way; and by night in a pillar of fire, to give them light; to go by day and night:

22 He took not away the pillar of the cloud by day, nor the pillar of fire by night, from before the people.

For a fleeting moment, Egypt's King begs the Children of Israel to leave. But this opportunity is short lived. The enemy will not give up without a fight. Moses leads the people of God, but it is actually the Lord God himself who is doing the leading with a pillar of cloud by day and a pillar of fire by night. This is emblematic of nothing other than the Spirit of God who leads and guides the newly liberated child of God. The people are ecstatic! Their faces beam with hope and faith as they gather their things and march out of town. But where is Moses taking them? There is still some unfinished business that must be taken care of.

The Lord God leads the people to the edge of the Red Sea. By this time Pharaoh has realized that the loss of his slave labor force will cripple the economy, and has set out in hot pursuit. With the armies of Egypt behind them, and the Sea before them, the Children of God seem to be trapped. Which way do they go? They can surrender and return to their bondage, or they can step out into the unknown guided only by the word of the One who says "Follow Me." Fortunately, they are not alone.

God has sovereignly decreed that it is by proclamation that his word goes forth, and that it is by hearing that this word takes effect. (Romans 10:14) The minister of

God (Moses) reminds them how they have obtained this freedom, and now urges them to hold on to this liberty and advance into areas of greater liberty. They can be rid of the slavers once and for all! This is not a suggestion that religious converts can move forward by their own effort. A sinner must repent for his own sin and must trust in the shed blood of his own Saviour, but he must also encounter the power of the living God.

Isaiah 53:10 Yet it pleased the LORD to bruise him; he hath put him to grief: when thou shalt make his soul an offering for sin, he shall see his seed, he shall prolong his days, and the pleasure of the LORD shall prosper in his hand.

11 He shall see of the travail of his soul, and shall be satisfied: by his knowledge shall my righteous servant justify many; for he shall bear their iniquities.

From the moment of conversion and liberation, the new believer is part of a great company of believers: a community of faith. There is also an immediate struggle for allegiance between the old way and the new way. God has a plan to sever the one from the other once and for all. The man of God is required to administer this work of grace.

Exodus 14:13 And Moses said unto the people, Fear ye not, stand still, and see the salvation of the LORD, which he will shew to you to day: for the Egyptians whom ye have seen to day, ye shall see them again no more for ever.

This step is bold, and public, and risky, and it will tend to separate a true believer from a pretender. The congregation still has its share of stealth believers who secretly desire to return to Egypt – some of them never wanted to leave in the first place. These troublemakers offer the misguided counsel that you can keep one foot in God's kingdom and the other foot in the Devil's domain.

But this is a lie! The enemy only enslaves and kills. There is no middle ground. There can be no compromise! Israel must move onward and upward!

Moses stretches out his rod, according to the word of the Lord, and the Red Sea opens up to make a way of escape for the people of God. The old man of sin goes into the water, and the new man of righteousness comes forth out of the water.

Exodus 14:21 And Moses stretched out his hand over the sea; and the LORD caused the sea to go back by a strong east wind all that night, and made the sea dry land, and the waters were divided.

22 And the children of Israel went into the midst of the sea upon the dry ground...

23 And the Egyptians pursued, and went in after them to the midst of the sea, even all Pharaoh's horses, his chariots, and his horsemen.

The power of the enemy is shattered. The power of God is triumphant! The body of death is buried, and the new man arises out of this watery grave to live a life of liberty and holiness unto the Lord.

Exodus 14:28 And the waters returned, and covered the chariots, and the horsemen, and all the host of Pharaoh that came into the sea after them; there remained not so much as one of them.

29 But the children of Israel walked upon dry land in the midst of the sea; and the waters were a wall unto them on their right hand, and on their left.

30 Thus the LORD saved Israel that day out of the hand of the Egyptians; and Israel saw the Egyptians dead upon the sea shore.

Even now, the journey has only begun. In the normal Christian experience that we read about in the Bible, a sinner repents and confesses his sin, throwing himself on the mercy of God based solely on the finished work of Jesus Christ. But the work of Jesus Christ did not end on the Cross. There was a grave to be reckoned with, and a resurrection to new life. A repentant believer will appropriate all of this finished work. Repentance is a real dying of the sinful man. Water baptism is a burial of the old man. Spirit baptism is a quickening of that dead man, bringing forth new life by the power of God. Then, by this same power the believer lives an overcoming life, faithful until he takes his rest. Physical death is outstripped by resurrection life that never ends. Eternal bliss is ours even now, by faith. The life of a believer is a life sustained by and nourished in the crucible of faith. Life on this planet is a pressure cooker, and the fires of our daily battle against sin try us and purge us of all self reliance and pride.

The pillars of cloud and fire continue to lead Israel day by day. At Mount Sinai the lawgiver teaches the people how to make their approach to a Holy God. These lessons include how to worship, how to enter in to the presence of God, and how to make amends for unintended and shameful transgressions. But what exactly is a transgression? At Sinai the Lord gives to his people the Ten Commandments, and Israel pledges to obey the Most High God.

The next stop on the path to the Promised Land is the river Jordan. The land of promise is none other than the land that was claimed by Abraham and Sarah as they walked to and fro in it. Theirs is a land of milk and honey, a place of safety and rest in the midst of a wicked generation, but it must be taken by force! The enemy never willingly vacates his land in order to make room for your destiny. There is a battle to fight and a war to win. Fortunately, the battle is the Lords, and he has already won the victory for us! (Psalm 98:1-3)

Moses sends a dozen spies into the land, hoping for a good report. Instead, all but two prove to be fearful and weak.

Numbers 13:27 And they told him, and said, We came unto the land whither thou sentest us, and surely it floweth with milk and honey; and this is the fruit of it.

28 Nevertheless the people be strong that dwell in the land, and the cities are walled, and very great: and moreover we saw the children of Anak there.

29 The Amalekites dwell in the land of the south: and the Hittites, and the Jebusites, and the Amorites, dwell in the mountains: and the Canaanites dwell by the sea, and by the coast of Jordan.

30 And Caleb stilled the people before Moses, and said, Let us go up at once, and possess it; for we are well able to overcome it.

Unbelief proves to be their undoing. The nation is doomed to wander in the wilderness until the entire generation is dead. Only Joshua and Caleb are allowed to enter the Promised Land. Faith is the key to an overcoming life, but faith in what or in whom? The 10 spies believed in the power of their enemies, as well as in the value of human reason. We, on the other hand, must believe the promise of God, regardless of how hopeless the circumstances might appear. The remaining and pivotal event in the story of the salvation of a people hinges on the presence and the power of God. There is no substitute for Holy Ghost Power. Human reasoning and good intentions will never serve to fulfill the plan and purpose of God in the life of a believing remnant. The making of an overcomer is a work that only God can accomplish.

Forty years later, the nation returns to the river Jordan. A new generation has emerged. They have no fond recollections of the old life in Egypt. They have heard the stories all their lives, and they look forward to the fulfillment. Some of them have vivid childhood memories of the walls of water and the destruction of the enemy army. They are not afraid. They are ready to occupy the land.

No man can take them forward from here. Moses is dead. Joshua cannot part the waters. The river is at flood stage. Only the presence and power of God can ferry them across the Jordan and unto a new life in the land of milk and honey.

A Three-Fold Cord

The Promised Land represents the Spirit-filled life of reliance on the abiding presence of God. We each have our battles to fight; our own victories to win. Yet the Lord of Hosts fights for us. (Exodus 14:14)

It is possible that Joshua would have liked to take the rod of Moses and part the river. I'm quite sure he understood the value of a symbolic gesture in the anointing of a leader and the forging of a political movement. Nevertheless, Joshua was obedient to the voice of the Spirit of God. This river of living water parts only when the presence of the Lord draws nigh.

Joshua 3:15 And as they that bare the ark were come unto Jordan, and the feet of the priests that bare the ark were dipped in the brim of the water, (for Jordan overfloweth all his banks all the time of harvest,)

16 That the waters which came down from above stood and rose up upon an heap very far from the city Adam, that is beside Zaretan: and those that came down toward the sea of the plain, even the salt sea, failed, and were cut off: and the people passed over right against Jericho.

17 And the priests that bare the ark of the covenant of the LORD stood firm on dry ground in the midst of Jordan, and all the Israelites passed over on dry ground, until all the people were passed clean over Jordan.

Crossing through Jordan is emblematic of a baptism in the Holy Ghost. (See John 7:37) And so we see that God is faithful to his word. The Exodus story clearly displays the salvation of God through Jesus Christ.

Phillip Stuckemeyer

The blood of the spotless lamb points to the crucifixion of messiah. The Red Sea crossing foreshadows the burial of the lifeless body of flesh. The crossing of the mighty river is a promise of the Holy Spirit that is ever present in and flowing through a redeemed people.

Blood, Water, and Spirit. Death, Burial, and Resurrection. Repentance, Water Baptism, and Spirit Baptism. The Children of Israel are only able to overcome by faith in the work of Jesus Christ at Calvary. It is the same in every generation.

Chapter 5

A Divine Pattern in the Heavenlies

Hebrews 8:1 ...We have such an high priest, who is set on the right hand of the throne of the Majesty...

2 A minister of the sanctuary, and of <u>the true tabernacle, which the Lord pitched</u>, and not man.

3 For every high priest is ordained to offer gifts and sacrifices...

5 Who serve unto <u>the example and shadow of heavenly things</u>, as Moses was admonished of God when he was about to make the tabernacle: for, See, saith he, that thou make all things <u>according to the pattern shewed to thee in the mount</u>.

The maker of heaven and earth is a God of order. This order is displayed openly in the creation by the many repetitive patterns that emerge during any serious study of the planet and its most basic elements. Science is the careful study of what is. While it is true that in our modern world there is much junk offered up as science by intellectually dishonest brokers of transformative change, there is still a solid technical foundation for the practice and the promotion of true science. True science is the systematic discovery of the creation as it actually exists in reality. Any serious attempt at uncovering the true nature of the fundamental fabric of the cosmos will result in a resounding heart's cry of "Abba, Father" since there is no other reasonable response for the creature who has come face to face with the reality of its Creator.

The scientific method demands that theory cannot be proven to be fact unless the evidence is observable and measurable based on solid data that is collected by experimental study and testing that yields valid and repeatable results in a controlled environment. To be truly scientific, the methodology used to arrive at a conclusion must also be objective, free of bias that may distort the result in favor of one predisposition or another. Examples of questionable science include the pronouncement by some that the theory of evolution is a fact, or that the globe is only warming due to excessive greenhouse gases. These are political and cultural statements that are intended to bend public opinion in favor of a specific agenda.

In stark contrast to the current wave of popular pseudo-scientific babble is the rock solid certainty of the truth. We who know God ought to boldly testify to the beauty and complexity of the creation within which we live and serve the Creator. The Bible not only declares that the reality of God is clearly evident in the environment, but that all environmentalists will ultimately bow their knees in humble submission to Father God rather than Mother Earth.

Romans 1:18 For the wrath of God is revealed from heaven against all ungodliness and unrighteousness of men, who hold the truth in unrighteousness;

19 Because that which may be known of God is manifest in them; for God hath shewed it unto them.

20 For the invisible things of him from the creation of the world are clearly seen, being understood by the things that are made, even his eternal power and Godhead; so that they are without excuse:

We would each do well to confess allegiance to God sooner rather than later, and there is no more compelling evidence to the existence of the God of the Bible than the remarkable consistency with which God exerts his sovereign influence upon a creation designed to show forth his glory. The Biblical narrative is brimming with rich and meaningful examples of God's showcasing of his plans and programs with technical detail and accuracy. Understandably, God requires that those servants whom he commissions to carry out his plans pay strict attention to detail. Let me give you a few examples:

When God commanded Noah to build an ark, he provided very specific design criteria. (See Genesis 6:14-16) As any shipbuilder will tell you, getting a vessel of that size to float with stability requires careful engineering and construction. How could Noah, who had never seen the rain, much less the awful power of a flood, possibly pull off such a massive shipbuilding effort on the first try? The answer is that God is the master architect, and that Noah paid attention to the details in the blueprint. In Matthew 24:33 we find a record of the Parable of the Fig Tree. Jesus makes the case in this passage that we will understand when we see all the details taking shape. But alas, Jesus explains in verses 37 thru 39, the last days will be just like Noah's day in that the majority of people will not be paying attention, and the disaster that catches them by surprise brings horrifying consequences.

Noah was paying attention, and was able to save not only his own household but the human race. Finally, in verse 43 Jesus makes it plain that if those responsible for standing guard had been paying attention, they would have seen the approaching disaster and would have been able to prepare for it.

The preparation of the Tabernacle of Moses is another example of the importance of attention to detail. God gave to Moses specific instructions on the construction and equipping of the Tabernacle in the wilderness. (Exodus Chap. 25-27) These instructions included the precise weaving of patterns into the fabrics that made up the tent-like structure, even requiring certain colors. (Exodus 26:31) Clearly God was making a statement, and was serious about the meanings of the many symbols and types that were illustrated in both the structure and the ritual practices of the Priests and Levites who attended to the Tabernacle. No detail was too small. Furthermore, God did not place his sovereign plan in jeopardy by allowing a group of self-willed men to interpret his plans any way they saw fit. Instead, God divinely endowed gifts and abilities on the craftsmen who were charged with actually building the Tabernacle; in effect inspiring them to be true to the original plan and purpose for it. (Exodus 35:30-35)

In Hebrews chapter 8 we see that the physical Tabernacle on the earth is merely an earthly representation of the true Tabernacle that is in the throne room of the Most High God. It is like a shadow that has the basic form and shape, but lacks the luster and the substance of that which is real. Jesus is the true Tabernacle, as is shown in John 1:14 where it is revealed that "The Word became flesh, and dwelt (literally tabernacled) among us." The Tabernacle of Moses was meant to show to the world in striking detail the salvation of God through the death, burial and resurrection of Jesus Christ. This was so important that God commanded Moses:

Exodus 25:9 According to all that I shew thee, after the pattern of the tabernacle, and the pattern of all the instruments thereof, even so shall ye make it.

We, too, must pay attention to the patterns revealed in Scripture. It is not possible to improve upon God's plan of salvation, and there is no other Saviour to whom we might turn.

Isaiah 45:20 Assemble yourselves and come; draw near together, ye that are escaped of the nations: they have no knowledge that set up the wood of their graven image, and pray unto a god that cannot save.

21 Tell ye, and bring them near; yea, let them take counsel together: who hath declared this from ancient time? who hath told it from that time? have not I the LORD? and there is no God else beside me; a just God and a Saviour; there is none beside me.

22 Look unto me, and be ye saved, all the ends of the earth: for I am God, and there is none else.

23 I have sworn by myself, the word is gone out of my mouth in righteousness, and shall not return, That unto me every knee shall bow, every tongue shall swear.

Chapter 6

The Tabernacle of Moses

Exodus 29:38 ...thou shalt <u>offer upon the altar; two lambs</u> of the first year day by day continually.

42 ...<u>a continual burnt offering</u> throughout your generations at the door of the tabernacle of the congregation before the LORD...

Exodus 40:30 <u>And he set the laver</u> between the tent of the congregation and the altar, <u>and put water there, to wash withal</u>.

32 When they went into the tent of the congregation, and when they came near unto the altar, <u>they washed; as the LORD commanded</u> Moses.

Hebrews 9:11 But Christ being come an high priest of good things to come, by a greater and more perfect tabernacle...

12 Neither by the blood of goats and calves, but <u>by his own blood he entered in once into the holy place</u>...

14 ...who <u>through the eternal Spirit offered himself without spot to God</u>...

A Three-Fold Cord

There are many, many books in circulation that detail the symbolic meaning of the various staves, and boards, and curtains, and pins, and furniture that make up the Tabernacle of Moses. There is no need for me to discuss these things, even though it might make for a fascinating Bible study. Instead, this book traces the Blood, and the Water, and the Spirit throughout the biblical narrative, and the Tabernacle plan is rich territory indeed. In this portable sanctuary that travelled with the Children of Israel wherever the Lord God chose to lead them, the salvation plan was dramatically reenacted day by day within view of the people. The smoke from the fires rose up continually as a beacon of hope to all the nations that surrounded the camp. Neither the Priest nor the common man fully understood the significance of the Tabernacle ritual; nevertheless, the daily sacrifice pre-figured the death, burial, and resurrection of Jesus Christ. Every man, woman, and child whose trust was exhibited through quiet obedience to the Word of God was accepted, and their simple, childlike faith was counted as righteousness.

The Tabernacle was arranged in such a way that the Priest on duty would progress from the low estate of the sinner into the presence of God. We all start at the same place, and are in need of the same redemption. The path to new life is the same path that was circuited day by day in the Tabernacle, and later the Temple that was based on the same template.

Shedding of Blood

The first stop for the sinner who needed forgiveness was the altar of burnt offering. Here the sinner confessed his sin publically. Even as the individual approached the Tabernacle, the people could see what sort of offering he brought, and they knew how severe a crime had been committed. The sinner brought with him an innocent animal, perhaps a lamb or a bullock, chosen carefully from among the flocks or the herds. It had to be the best. Nothing less would do. Forgiveness of sins is not a trifling matter. God demands heart-felt sincerity and repentance from the guilty party. While the sinner stood beside the substitute, the sin was ceremonially transferred to the innocent, the throat was cut, and the life was drained. The blood of the sacrifice was caught in a basin and sprinkled upon the altar. (Leviticus 7:2) It was a horrifying and bloody business. The innocent paid the ultimate price. The guilty went free.

The Priest would prepare the sacrifice and offer it upon the altar of burnt offering. The entire process was difficult and dirty work. The unclean portion was carried without the camp, the burnt offering was placed upon the fire, and a portion was laid aside to provide for the Levites and their families. When the work was finished, the priest was contaminated by the blood and filth.

Washing in Water

Nothing unclean can enter into the presence of a Holy God. The Tabernacle Priest was not exempt from this rule. Tainted by the filth and corruption of sin, his next stop was the brazen Laver. Made of highly polished brass, the Priest could see his reflection as he approached. He could see how dirty he was before washing, and he could step back and examine himself again after washing. The Laver was continually being filled with clean water, and the Priest would wash away the blood and the filth of sin and death before continuing into the Holy Place.

Entering by Spirit

Inside the tent, in that section of the Tabernacle known as The Holy Place, were prominently placed three articles of furniture. To the left stood a Golden Candlestick. To the right sat a Table of Shewbread. Straight ahead, an Altar of Incense was just outside the Most Holy Place. Continually tended by the Aaronic Priesthood, these articles were rich in symbolic meaning.

The Golden Candlestick was kept burning at all times. The oil for the lamps is representative of the Spirit of God. The light that shined from the lamps both illuminated the way and drove out the darkness. The need to continually replenish the oil for the lamps speaks of our need for the frequent and continual refilling of the Holy Spirit. The illumination of the Holy Spirit makes it possible for us to see clearly, and to find our way into the presence of God, rather than groping in the darkness.

At the Table of Shewbread, the Priest partook of the fresh, unleavened bread. The Bread of Life is the Word of God, and speaks of our daily need for reading, studying, and meditating upon the Bible. The absence of leaven stands for the pure, unadulterated Word of God, free from hypocrisy and the pride that so easily "Puffs Up" the empty, shallow, religious adherent.

At the Altar of Incense, the Priest perpetually tended to the burning of sweet incense, a continual offering of a sweet smelling fragrance unto the Lord. The smoke that arose from the Altar of Incense speaks of the prayers and the praise of the people of God that were offered up continually at the Throne of Grace.

The Presence and Power of God

Beyond the Veil in the Holy of Holies resided the Ark of the Covenant that bore the Mercy Seat. Though the Priests drew near day by day, the High Priest only entered beyond the Veil once a year to atone for the sins of the nation. The Veil was a "wall of separation" that protected a sinful people from the severity of a Holy God, and prevented the people from defiling the symbolic dwelling place of the One who is always present in every place.

The Way to God

The Tabernacle ritual was a daily prophetic proclamation of the promise of God to save sinners by the Death, Burial, and Resurrection of Jesus the Messiah. Faithful obedience was nothing less than faith in the substitutionary sacrifice of the Lamb of God. This was, and has always been, the only way to draw near to God: Faith in Jesus Christ is the message of the Tabernacle.

Abraham, Moses, David, you and I can only be saved by trusting in Jesus.

Hebrews 10:22 Let us draw near with a true heart in full assurance of faith, having our hearts sprinkled from an evil conscience, and our bodies washed with pure water.

Chapter 7

The Only Way to God

Hebrews 10:19 Having therefore, brethren, boldness to <u>enter into the holiest by the blood of Jesus</u>,

20 <u>By a new and living way</u>...

21 And having an high priest over the house of God;

22 <u>Let us draw near with a true heart in full assurance of faith, having our hearts sprinkled from an evil conscience, and our bodies washed with pure water</u>.

23 Let us hold fast the profession of our faith without wavering...

The Hebrew experience is unique. Although modern Jewish orthodoxy is heavily steeped in tradition and has been profoundly influenced by Babylonian mystery religions, it was once the pure worship of Yahweh. In fact, I would suggest that the religion of Moses and David is the only true religion that has ever existed on planet earth.

I am aware that such a statement is charged with implications about the other religions of the world, including the Christian religions. I also realize that my position will not be popular in our pluralistic society. A survey of the doctrinal beliefs and practices of mainline Christian denominations quickly reveals a wide variety of questionable liturgical rituals. Many of these rituals can be traced back to the same Babylonian mysteries that transformed the pure religion of the Children of Israel into something that Aaron (the brother of Moses, who was also the first High Priest in the original Tabernacle) would scarcely recognize.

We should not be surprised to find that superstition and mythology abounded in the early human civilizations, but it is unfortunate. Immediately after man's fall into sin we find a record of the sinner's attempts to approach a holy God. Consider what Matthew Henry's Concise Commentary on the Bible has to say about the story of Cain and Abel that was recorded in Genesis chapter 4.

> We may believe that God commanded Adam, after the fall, to shed the blood of innocent animals, and after their death to burn part or the whole of their bodies by fire. Thus that punishment which sinners deserve, even the death of the body, and the wrath of God, of which fire is a well-known emblem, and also the sufferings of Christ, were prefigured. Observe that the religious worship of God is no new invention. It was from the beginning; it is the good old way (Jeremiah 6:16). The offerings of Cain and Abel were different. Cain showed a proud, unbelieving heart. Therefore he and his offering were rejected. Abel came as a sinner, and according to God's appointment, by his sacrifice expressing humility, sincerity, and believing obedience. Thus, seeking the benefit of the new covenant of mercy, through the promised Seed, his sacrifice had a token that God

accepted it. Abel offered in faith, and Cain did not (Hebrews 11:4). In all ages there have been two sorts of worshippers, such as Cain and Abel; namely, proud, hardened despisers of the gospel method of salvation, who attempt to please God in ways of their own devising; and humble believers, who draw near to him in the way he has revealed. Cain indulged malignant anger against Abel. He harboured an evil spirit of discontent and rebellion against God. God notices all our sinful passions and discontents. There is not an angry, envious, or fretful look, that escapes his observing eye. The Lord reasoned with this rebellious man; if he came in the right way, he should be accepted. Some understand this as an intimation of mercy. "If thou doest not well, sin, that is, the sin-offering, lies at the door, and thou mayest take the benefit of it." The same word signifies sin, and a sacrifice for sin. "Though thou hast not done well, yet do not despair; the remedy is at hand." Christ, the great sin-offering, is said to stand at the door (Revelation 3:20). And those well deserve to perish in their sins, that will not go to the door to ask for the benefit of this sin-offering.

Since the Bible doesn't record exactly what the Lord God told Adam about how to worship or pray, there is a good bit of speculation put forward by Matthew Henry. But this sort of conjecture is not at all unreasonable. What should be abundantly clear to us is that there is a tendency among sinful men to reject the counsel of God and to invent their own method of reaching for the heavens. The Tower of Babel (Genesis 11) is a notable example of such tendencies.

The Children of Israel were surrounded by pagan, polytheistic nations who were hostile towards God. The Tabernacle in the wilderness stood in stark contrast to their counterfeit temples and shrines. It should be no surprise to us that the pagan nations both feared and disliked the Hebrews. Even today, any suggestion that a particular belief system or lifestyle choice is misguided or ungodly evokes an immediate charge of intolerance or hatred, and sometimes even racial bias or prejudice.

The Tabernacle travelled with the people of God, and was a visible reminder to all that Almighty God dwells in the midst of his people. The gods of the nations were no gods at all, and were really only a tribute to the pride of sinful men. A universal consequence of sin is the separation of the unclean from the holy, and the ceremonial and dietary customs of the Mosaic Law were an essential part of God's plan to preserve a righteous bloodline that would bring forth the promised savior. Wicked men bristle at the thought that they need a savior. Even in our modern society the secular religion of Humanism proclaims that man is capable of rescuing himself, and rejects the existence of a supreme deity. Naturally, they believe that there are an unlimited variety of paths to eternal life, though they often aren't sure what that means.

There are many people who believe that there is more than one way to God. You would expect such a thing from the religions of the world, but you may be surprised to find that even among evangelical Christians there are those who believe that God has made more than one way to obtain salvation.

One rather novel doctrine that has taken the church world by storm is Dispensational Pre-Millennialism. The most familiar token of this eschatological school of thought is the famous "Rapture of the Church" which offers to believers the hope that they will escape tribulation and persecution in the last days by being "caught away" before the going gets too tough.

The major problem with this doctrine, in my opinion, is that you must allow for different salvation plans during different dispensations of time.

Some of my friends, and probably many of my readers, do not believe that this is true. One friend told me that I was the only person he knows who thinks this is what dispensationalists believe, and he himself is a dispensationalist. It may be helpful, then, if I borrow a quote from an authoritative source. Anthony A. Hoekema (1913-1988) was a professor of systematic theology at Calvin Theological Seminary in Grand Rapids, Michigan. The following overview of the doctrine, including quotes from dispensational experts (sources cited on page 53) was taken from his book titled *The Bible and the Future.*

> Dispensationalists divide God's dealings with humanity into a number of distinct "dispensations." The *New Scofield Bible* distinguishes seven such dispensations: Innocence, Conscience or Moral Responsibility, Human Government, Promise, Law, the Church, and the Kingdom. A dispensation is defined as "a period of time during which man is tested in respect to his obedience to some specific revelation of the will of God." [43] Though in each dispensation God reveals his will in a different way, these dispensations are not separate ways of salvation. "During each of them [the dispensations] man is reconciled to God in only one way, i.e. by God's grace through the work of Christ that was accomplished on the cross and vindicated in his resurrection." [44] The dispensation of the Kingdom is the millennial reign of Christ, which will occur after his return.

The Old Testament contains many promises that, some time

A Three-Fold Cord

in the future, God will establish an earthly kingdom involving the people of Israel, his ancient covenant people. Though the Abrahamic covenant included promises to the spiritual seed of Abraham, its central promise was that Abraham's physical descendants would be given the land of Canaan as an everlasting possession. In the Davidic covenant the promise was given that one of David's descendants (namely, the coming Messiah) would sit forever upon David's throne, ruling over the people of Israel. The new covenant predicted in Jeremiah 31:31-34, though including certain features which are already being fulfilled for believers in the present Church Age, is essentially a covenant for Israel, which will not be completely fulfilled until the time of the coming millennium. A great many passages in the Psalms and prophets (e.g., Ps. 72:1-20; Isa. 2:1-4; 11:1-9, 11-16; 65:18-25; Jer. 23:5-6; Amos 9:11-15; Mic. 4:1-4; Zech. 14:1-9, 16-21) predict that the people of Israel will at some future time once again be regathered in the land of Canaan, will enjoy a time of prosperity and blessing, will have a special place of privilege above other nations, and will live under the benevolent and perfect rule of their Messiah, the descendant of David. Since none of these promises has yet been fulfilled, dispensationalists expect them to be fulfilled during Christ's millennial reign.

When Christ was on earth, he offered the kingdom of heaven to the Jews of his day. This kingdom was to be an earthly rule over Israel, in fulfillment of Old Testament prophecies; entrance into the kingdom, moreover, would require repentance for sin, faith in Jesus as the Messiah, and a willingness to adopt the high standard of morality taught, for example, in the Sermon on the Mount. The Jews at that time, however, rejected the kingdom. The final establishment of this kingdom, therefore, was now postponed until the time of the millennium. In the meantime, Christ introduced the "mystery form" of the kingdom—a form described in such parables as those of the Sower and the Tares in Matthew 13. An exponent of this view, E. Schuyler English, puts it this way: "The kingdom in mystery is Christendom, that portion of the world where the name of Christ is professed. It is the visible church, composed of unbelievers as well as believers, that constitutes the kingdom of heaven in mystery. It will continue till the end of the age, when Christ will return to the earth to reign as King." [45]

Since the kingdom in its final or "real" form had been rejected by the Jews, Christ now proceeded to establish the church. The purpose of the church is to gather believers, primarily Gentiles but inclusive of Jews, as the body of Christ—a gathering or "calling out" which will not be completed until Christ comes again for the rapture. Though the Davidic kingdom was predicted in the Old Testament, the church was not. The church therefore constitutes a kind of "parenthesis" in the plan of God, interrupting God's predicted program for Israel. "… The present age [the Church Age] is a parenthesis or a time period not predicted by the Old Testament and therefore not fulfilling or advancing the program of events revealed in the Old Testament foreview." [46]

Christ's return, as we saw above,[47] will occur in two stages or phases. The first phase will be the so-called rapture, which can occur at any moment. Here an important difference between pretribulational dispensational premillennialism and historic premillennialism emerges; whereas the latter looks for certain signs of the times to be fulfilled before Christ returns, the former expects these signs to be fulfilled after the first phase of the return has occurred. Pretribulational dispensationalists, in other words, believe in the so-called *imminent* or *any-moment* coming of Christ.[48] At the time of the rapture Christ does not come all the way down to the earth, but only part of the way. Now the resurrection of all true believers, exclusive of Old Testament saints, takes place. After this resurrection believers who are still alive—believing Jews as well as believing Gentiles—shall suddenly be transformed and glorified. Now the rapture of all of God's people occurs; risen believers and transformed believers are caught up in the clouds to meet the descending Lord in the air. This body of believers, called the church, now goes up to the heaven with Christ to celebrate with him for seven years the marriage feast of the Lamb.

The seven-year period which follows is a fulfillment of the seventieth week of Daniel's prophecy (Dan. 9:24-27). Dispensationalists hold that though the sixty-ninth week of this prophecy was fulfilled at the time of Christ's first coming, the prophecy about the seventieth week (v. 27) will not be fulfilled until after the rapture. During this seven-year period, while the church remains in heaven, a number of events will occur on earth: (1) the tribulation predicted in Daniel 9:27 now begins, the latter half of which is the so-called *great tribulation*; (2) the antichrist now begins his cruel reign—a reign which culminates in his demanding to be worshiped as God; (3) terrible judgments now fall on the inhabitants of the earth; (4) at this time a remnant of Israel will turn to Jesus as the Messiah — the 144,000 sealed Israelites of Revelation 7:3-8; (5) this remnant of Israel will now begin to preach the "Gospel of the Kingdom" — a gospel having as its central content the establishment of the coming Davidic kingdom, but including the message of the cross and the need for faith and repentance; (6) through the witness of this Jewish remnant an innumerable multitude of Gentiles will also be brought to salvation (Rev. 7:9); (7) the kings of the earth and the armies of the beast and the false prophet now gather together to attack the people of God in the Battle of Armageddon.

Please allow me to interrupt Dr. Hoekema for a moment. Dispensationalism's treatment of this seven-year period comes dangerously close to allowing salvation by works. Some adherents to this novel doctrine insist that those "left behind" after the "rapture" still gain access to the grace of God in the same manner as all other believers, that is, by faith in Jesus. Other proponents of this view suggest that salvation cannot occur in a normal fashion since the Holy Spirit left the planet along with the "raptured" saints. If you have never encountered this idea, let me quote a few lines from Dr. Kelley Varner's book *Whose Right It Is – A*

Phillip Stuckemeyer

Handbook of Covenantal Theology (Shippensburg: Destiny Image, 1975) in which he discusses 2 Thessalonians 2:7.

> The word for "letteth" and "let" here in Second Thessalonians 2:7 is the same as "withholdeth" in verse 6. "Only" (but) he who now "restrains" will "restrain" until… Until what? "Until he be taken out of the way."

> As noted, dispensationalists use this strange expression of Second Thessalonians 2:7 to say that the "restrainer" is the Holy Spirit (in all believers), who shall be "taken" out of the way when the Church is raptured from the earth (also citing Mt. 24:37-41). The major problem with that supposition is that no man can be saved (during a future tribulation period or any other time) without the Holy Spirit (Jn. 6:44)!

Admittedly, neither Drs. Hoekema nor Varner adhere to this system of dispensational eschatology, but both are trustworthy scholars who provide a balanced summary of this end time view. Though the doctrine is fatalistic at its core, it has also proven to be a fantastic marketing tool. Millions of books and videos have been sold to pampered churchgoers who are willing to spend money for the latest magic pills, potions, get rich quick schemes and other escapist paraphernalia. But why are they so eager to abandon the earth to its greatest enemy? Historically, the church has always triumphed over its persecutors during the times of tribulation the Lord Jesus promised we would face (see John 16:33.) It is time to return our focus to Hoekema's book, *The Bible and the Future*.

> At the end of the seven-year period Christ will return in glory, accompanied by the church. At this time he will come all the way down to earth and will destroy his enemies, thus ending the Battle of Armageddon. By this time the nation of Israel will have

been regathered into Palestine. When Christ returns, the vast majority of Israelites then living will turn to Christ in faith and be saved, in fulfillment of Old and New Testament predictions. The devil will now be bound, cast into the abyss, and sealed there for a thousand years—the time period is understood in a strictly literal way. Saints who died during the seven-year tribulation which has just ended are now raised from the dead (Rev. 20:4); the resurrection of Old Testament saints also occurs at this time. These resurrected saints, however, will not enter the millennial kingdom which is about to be established; they will join the risen and translated saints who constitute the raptured church in heaven. Now follows the judgment of living Gentiles, recorded in Matthew 25:31-46. This judgment concerns not nations but individuals. "The test of this judgment will be how individual Gentiles treated Christ's brethren—whether brethren according to the flesh (i.e. Jews) or brethren according to the Spirit (i.e. saved people)—during the 'tribulation.' " [49] The sheep—those who pass the test—will be left on earth to enter the millennial kingdom. The goats—those who fail to pass the test—will be cast into everlasting fire. Next follows the judgment upon Israel, mentioned in Ezekiel 20:33-38. The rebels among the Israelites will be put to death at this time and will not be permitted to enjoy the blessings of the millennium. Those Israelites who have turned to the Lord, however, will enter the millennial reign and will enjoy its blessings.

Christ now begins his millennial reign. He ascends a throne in Jerusalem and rules over a kingdom which is primarily Jewish, though Gentiles also share its blessings; the Jews, however, are exalted above the Gentiles. At the beginning of the millennium Christ rules over those who have survived the judgment of the Gentiles and the judgment of Israel just described. Those who are members of the millennial kingdom, therefore, are not resurrected believers, but believers who were still living when Christ returned for the second phase of his Second Coming; it should also be noted that at the beginning of the millennium no unregenerate people are living on the earth. The millennial reign of Christ fulfills the promises made to Israel in the Old Testament: "The earthly purpose of Israel of which dispensationalists speak concerns the national promise which will be fulfilled by Jews during the millennium as they live on the earth in *un*resurrected bodies. The earthly future for Israel does not concern Israelites who die before the millennium is set up." [50]

Those who enter the millennial kingdom will be normal human beings. They will marry and reproduce, and most of them will die. The millennium will be a time of prosperity, marvelous productivity, and peace; it will be a golden age such as the world has never seen before. The earth will be full of the knowledge of God as the waters cover the sea. Worship in the millennium will center around a rebuilt temple in Jerusalem, to which all nations will go to offer praise to God. Animal sacrifices will once again be offered at the temple. These sacrifices, however, will not be propitiatory offerings, but memorial offerings, in remembrance of Christ's death for us.

Here, then, we see another way in which dispensationalism comes perilously close to an alternative salvation plan. What seems to be a rather strange menu of faith, animal sacrifice and religious ritual is offered as standard fare in the Millennium Temple Café. And to make the drama even stranger, today's most cynical Bible teachers are encouraging their students to hope for an acceleration of the "signs of the times" which are also known as the "time of Jacob's trouble" as a means of hastening the march on Jerusalem and shortening the secret rapture timetable. A Pentecostal preacher and cattle grower named Clyde Lott is even trying to breed a herd of Red Heifers that can be used in the ritual cleansing necessary for the reestablishment of Temple worship. You can search Google for this information. But now, back to Hoekema!

What will be the relation of resurrected saints to the millennial earth? Resurrected saints will be living in the new, heavenly

A Three-Fold Cord

Jerusalem which is described in Revelation 21:1-22:5. During the millennial reign this heavenly Jerusalem will be in the air above the earth, shedding its light upon the earth. Resurrected saints will play some part in the millennial reign, since they will participate with Christ in certain judgments (cf. Matt. 19:28; I Cor. 6:2; and Rev. 20:6). It would appear, therefore, that resurrected saints are able to descend from the New Jerusalem to the earth in order to engage in these judgments. These judging activities, however, seem to be "limited to a few specific functions, and the primary activity of the resurrected saints will be in the new and heavenly city." [51]

Though at the beginning of the millennium only regenerate people are living on the earth, the children born to these people during the millennium will in time far outnumber their parents. Many of these children will be converted and become true believers. Those who turn out to be rebellious against the Lord will be kept in check by Christ and, if necessary, put to death. Those who merely profess the Christian faith but are not true believers will be gathered together by Satan at the end of the millennium (after he has been loosed from his prison) for a final attack against the "camp of the saints." This final revolt, however, will be totally crushed by Christ, God's enemies will be destroyed, and Satan will be cast into the lake of fire. Before the millennium ends, all believers who died during the millennium will be raised.

After the millennium has ended, all the unbelieving dead will be raised and will be judged before the great white throne. Since their names have not been written in the book of life, they will all be cast into the lake of fire, which is the second death.

The final state will now be ushered in. God will now create a new heaven and a new earth, from which all sin and imperfection will have been removed. The heavenly Jerusalem, the dwelling place of resurrected saints, will now descend to this new earth, where God and his people will dwell together in perfect bliss everlastingly. Though the people of God on the new earth will

> be one, there will remain a distinction throughout all eternity between redeemed Jews and redeemed Gentiles.
>
> The relation between the fulfillment of God's promises to the nation of Israel during the millennium and the final destiny of saved individual Israelites is indicated in the following quotation: "... The Old Testament held forth a national hope, which will be realized fully in the millennial age. The individual Old Testament saint's hope of an eternal city will be realized through resurrection in the heavenly Jerusalem, where, without losing distinction or identity, Israel will join with the resurrected and translated of the church age to share in the glory of His [Christ's] reign forever." [52]

Most dispensationalists agree with me that, before the crucifixion, salvation was <u>never</u> by careful obedience of the Law, but rather by faith in the promised future Messiah. This common ground vanishes when the last days come into view. This book is not about the last days, but about the only salvation plan God has offered to a sinful human race. From ancient times there have been many pagan religions offering false hope to a doomed and despondent world. The salvation that God promised to Adam and Eve is the only true hope available throughout the ages. In more recent times (The rapture doctrine was first taught in 1830.) the enemy has changed tactics. Let me quote Dr. Varner one last time.

> The dragon is defeated, but he still has a mouth. His purpose is to abort the Seed of Abraham and David, to keep the church in the dark as to her true covenantal identity in Christ. To this end, the god of this world invented dispensationalism in all its forms. Interestingly, every major false religion in America began to evolve and develop at the *same time*.

1. Mormonism — Joseph Smith organized the "Church of Jesus Christ of Latter-Day Saints" in 1830.
2. Seventh-Day Adventism — Following William Miller's false predictions of 1843-44, the S.D.A. Church was organized in 1860. It was later led by Ellen G. White.
3. Spiritism — Beginning with the Fox sisters in 1847, the "National Spiritualist Association of the U.S. of A." was formed in 1863.
4. Christian Science — Mary Baker Eddy published her bible, *Science and Health*, in 1875.
5. Jehovah's Witnesses — Charles Taze Russell published the first issue of *The Watchtower* in 1879.

To distract men from the genuine Pentecostal outpouring of the Spirit (1900-1910), the devil attempted to counterfeit and prostitute New Testament realities. One of his most powerful tools was the futurism found in the notes of Scofield's bible (1909).

My purpose in this rather lengthy chapter has been to substantiate my concern that many Bible teachers and therefore many Bible believing Christians have been duped into a modern belief system that makes unnecessary allowances for innovative and alternative paths to eternal life. The Bible clearly teaches only one way to God. If you are sympathetic to the claims of dispensationalism, I would only urge you to be sure that you really know the historical roots of all doctrines that you embrace. Trust in Jesus alone!

Hoekema's Footnotes

43. *New Scofield Bible*, p. 3 n. 3.
44. *Ibid.*
45. *A Companion to the New Scofield Reference Bible*, p. 97.

Phillip Stuckemeyer

46. Walvoord, *Kingdom*, p. 231.
47. See above, pp. 164-65.
48. Midtribulationists, who hold that the church will be raptured in the midst of the tribulation, and posttribulationists, who affirm that the church will be raptured at the end of the tribulation, do not accept the "any-moment coming" theory, since they look for certain signs to be fulfilled before the rapture occurs.
49. English, op. cit., p. 150.
50. Charles C. Ryrie, *Dispensationalism Today*, p. 146.
51. Walvoord, *Kingdom*, p. 329. On the role of the heavenly Jerusalem during the millennium see also Pentecost, *Things to Come*, pp. 563-80.
52. Pentecost, *Things to Come*, p. 546.

Anthony Hoekema, The Bible and the Future © 1994 Wm. B. Eerdmans Publishing Company, Grand Rapids, MI. Reprinted by permission of the publisher; all rights reserved.

Chapter 8

The Sign of the Prophet Jonah

Matthew 12:38 Then certain of the scribes and of the Pharisees answered, saying, Master, we would see a sign from thee.

39 But he answered and said unto them, An evil and adulterous generation seeketh after a sign; and there shall no sign be given to it, but <u>the sign of the prophet Jonas</u>:

40 <u>For as Jonas was three days and three nights in the whale's belly; so shall the Son of man be three days and three nights in the heart of the earth</u>.

Some people think that the Old Testament is little more than a collection of interesting stories, fanciful history, and exotic poetry. What they often fail to realize is that the stories were carefully designed to lay a prophetic foundation for the coming of the King of Kings. Jesus often referred to these stories as he proclaimed that the Kingdom of God was manifest. On one occasion the religious hypocrites demanded that he authenticate his ministry and his message with some spectacular sign or miracle. He referred them to the book of Jonah.

Yes, Jonah was rebellious, but that is not the point. Jonah's adventure was sovereignly appointed to show forth the death, burial and resurrection of the coming Messiah.

Death

Jonah willingly sacrificed himself to salvage the lives of his companions and shipmates. (See Jonah 1:12 and 1:15)

Burial

Having been swallowed up by a great fish that had been prepared by God, Jonah was in the depths of the sea, out of sight, for a total of three days and three nights. (See Jonah 1:17 and 2:2-6)

Resurrection

Right on time, the fish spit Jonah up onto the beach. He emerged with a new lease on life, and went forth in the power of God to declare the day of the Lord. (See Jonah 2:10 and Jonah 3)

Summary

Jesus tells us the real purpose for which the book of Jonah was recorded in the scripture - so that the generation to whom he preached would recognize him as the fulfillment of the perfect will of the God of Israel. Fulfilled prophecy is rock solid evidence, and Jesus corroborates the testimony of the Prophet Jonah who pointed the Jews to a savior who:

- o would be put to death,
- o would lie in the tomb for 3 days, but
- o would ultimately be raised from the dead in complete victory over his enemies.

Chapter 9

A Voice Crying in the Wilderness

John the Baptist

Matthew 3:1 In those days came John the Baptist, preaching...

2 And saying, <u>Repent ye</u>: for the kingdom of heaven is at hand.

7 But when he saw many of the Pharisees and Sadducees come to his baptism, he said unto them, O generation of vipers, who hath warned you to flee from the wrath to come?

8 Bring forth therefore fruits meet for repentance:

11 <u>I indeed baptize you with water unto repentance</u>. but he that cometh after me is mightier than I... <u>he shall baptize you with the Holy Ghost, and with fire</u>:

John was the cousin of the Lord Jesus, and was miraculously conceived 6 months before Jesus so that he could be a forerunner. He charged the people to prepare for the coming of Messiah.

"The voice of him that crieth in the wilderness," the work of John the Baptist had been foretold by the Prophet Isaiah. (40:3) The prophet said John would speak comfortably to the people of God, declaring that the time was come for their iniquity to be pardoned, and that the glory of the Lord was about to be revealed. As such, reasonable people would expect his message to be fully consistent with God's salvation plan.

Repentance

John insisted that the people sincerely repent of their sins. Such repentance would be authenticated by actions. For a sinner, this requirement entails a death of the old man. A turning away from the flesh is a turning unto God who offers hope and a fresh start.

Water Baptism

Ceremonial washing was commonplace in the Jewish religious culture. John emphasized that this washing was different, and he rebuked the hypocrites who came to the river without repentance. When there is no true change of heart, the dry sinner merely gets wet. Death is followed by burial: the corpse of sin is hidden away. The miracle that follows is that the dead is raised up to a new life.

Spirit Baptism

John pointed the people to the Lamb of God who would take away their sins. This mighty work would

Phillip Stuckemeyer

not be mere symbolism. Jesus would immerse them in Holy Ghost power. Little did they know the meaning of these words. Tragically, many still don't know about the baptism of the Holy Ghost!

Section 2

Messiah's Fulfillment

Luke 24:44 And he said unto them, These are the words which I spake unto you, while I was yet with you, that <u>all things must be fulfilled, which were written</u> in the law of Moses, and in the prophets, and in the psalms, concerning me.

45 Then opened he their understanding, that they might understand the scriptures,

46 And said unto them, <u>Thus it is written, and thus it behooved Christ to suffer, and to rise from the dead the third day</u>:

The Bible is a collection of books about Jesus Christ. Cover to cover, from the first page of Genesis to the last page of Revelation, every word and every idea is focused on Messiah.

Even those obscure passages that do not seem to be about Jesus do, in fact, concern him. This is what Jesus said in Luke 24:44, as is further substantiated in the Gospel according to John.

John 5:38 And ye have not his word abiding in you: for whom he hath sent, him ye believe not.

39 Search the scriptures; for in them ye think ye have eternal life: and they are they which testify of me.

40 And ye will not come to me, that ye might have life.

Jesus Christ is the fulfillment of the Holy Scriptures. He is not merely the subject of the book, but is literally The Word of God in fleshly form. The Bible refers to Jesus as:

1. the Word (John 1:1, John 1:14)
2. the Voice of the Lord (Genesis 3:8, Acts 7:31)
3. the Image of the Invisible God (Colossians 1:15)
4. the Expression of God's Person (Hebrews 1:3)

So it is that all the Law, and the Prophets, and the Psalms must be fulfilled. Not a single word must fail.

Matthew 5:18 For verily I say unto you, Till heaven and earth pass, one jot or one tittle shall in no wise pass from the law, till all be fulfilled.

If this seems unreasonable or impossible, it is only because we lack understanding. It is not only the uneducated or the illiterate that need to be enlightened. The Bible makes it clear that, absent a spiritual encounter with the living God, a natural man can never comprehend the meaning of the scriptures.

1 Corinthians 2:14 But the natural man receiveth not the things of the Spirit of God: for they are foolishness unto him: neither can he know them, because they are spiritually discerned.

Chapter 10

The Life of Jesus

Hebrews 4:14 Seeing then that we have a great high priest, that is passed into the heavens, <u>Jesus</u> the Son of God, let us hold fast our profession.

15 For we have not an high priest which cannot be touched with the feeling of our infirmities; but <u>was in all points tempted like as we are, yet without sin</u>.

16 <u>Let us therefore come boldly</u> unto the throne of grace, that we may obtain mercy, <u>and find grace</u> to help in time of need.

The Bible does not say a lot about the first thirty years of the life of Jesus. It does accurately chronicle his conception, birth, and the persecution of Herod. His coming of age is recorded, and his early devotion to his heavenly Father's business, as well as his submission to the authority of his earthly father and mother. At age 30, however, the young man is qualified for service in the Priesthood, and he enters public life and ministry in a manner that is probably best described as "Suddenly!"

Malachi 3:1 Behold, I will send my messenger, and he shall prepare the way before me: and the LORD, whom ye seek, shall suddenly come to his temple, even the messenger of the covenant, whom ye delight in: behold, he shall come, saith the LORD of hosts.

John the Baptist was the messenger who announced the coming of the Messiah with no small amount of fanfare. Jesus did not appear in fancy clothing, with regal attendants and a mighty army, but not because he lacked for such glory. The army of heaven was encamped about him, watching intently as the perfect will of God was accomplished. The will of God was that Jesus would take our place, and pay our penalty. It would ordinarily have been no challenge for the Lord of Glory to deal with the rigors of life on planet earth. Roman rule did not intimidate him one bit. Even the matter of crucifixion would have seemed no more severe than a mosquito bite were it not for the fact that Jesus willingly divested himself of the advantages of deity during his sojourn on the third planet from the sun. In order for him to truly taste death, with all of its horrors, he found it necessary to first subject himself to the fleshly limitations that are the common experience of every man.

Jesus knows what we face, because he faced it with us and for us. He was perfect; entirely without sin, and yet he voluntarily gave himself to hunger, weakness, loneliness, ridicule, humiliation, pain, suffering, and death. He was tempted in every way known to man, and yet he triumphed over sin. (Hebrews 4:15)

Though Jesus was not in need of forgiveness, he did find

it necessary to submit himself to the ministry of John the Baptist, if for no other reason than to show us the way that leads to life.

Repentance

John preached "Repent, for the kingdom of heaven is at hand." Jesus did not need to repent, for he had committed no sin. Nevertheless, at the appointed time, Jesus came to the Jordan and presented himself to John the Baptist. It is not clear from the scripture that John had ever been acquainted with Jesus during childhood, but while they were both in the womb John leaped for joy at the very presence of Jesus. (See Luke 1:44) As Jesus made his approach to the Jordan, the Baptist was stunned. John knew full well which of them was the filthy sinner. He knew that he himself needed to be cleansed by Jesus.

Matthew 3:13 Then cometh Jesus from Galilee to Jordan unto John, to be baptized of him.

14 But John forbad him, saying, I have need to be baptized of thee, and comest thou to me?

Repentance has always been the starting place for sinners who must stand before a holy God. It was so under the law, and it continues to be so under grace. Nothing has changed, as far as God is concerned. He has merely moved his plan forward another step. Men must still make a choice. Jesus is showing us that we must respond to the Gospel. Reject it or receive it. There can be no neutral parties in such a transaction between God and men.

Luke 16:13 No servant can serve two masters: for

either he will hate the one, and love the other; or else he will hold to the one, and despise the other. Ye cannot serve God and mammon.

14 And the Pharisees also, who were covetous, heard all these things: and they derided him.

15 And he said unto them, Ye are they which justify yourselves before men; but God knoweth your hearts: for that which is highly esteemed among men is abomination in the sight of God.

16 The law and the prophets were until John: since that time the kingdom of God is preached, and every man presseth into it.

17 And it is easier for heaven and earth to pass, than one tittle of the law to fail.

Jesus unequivocally sets forth the principle that the appearance of John the Baptist signaled an abrupt change in the Kingdom of God. The familiar religious forms were about to be abandoned, though the substance would remain, and even be more firmly established.

Repentance is the only appropriate response to the preaching of the Gospel of Jesus Christ. It most certainly is not optional.

<u>Water Baptism</u>

Since Jesus was not tainted by the effects of sin, he therefore had no need of a ceremonial cleansing. He wasn't dirty, and so he did not need to be washed. But baptism in water is more than a bath. This immersion into water signals the burial of a man who is fully and finally dead to trespasses and sins.

Romans 6:4 Therefore we are buried with him by baptism into death: that like as Christ was raised up from the dead by the glory of the Father, even so we also should walk in newness of life.

The burial into the watery grave is followed by a coming forth from the same grave. The ultimate result of water baptism is not that the sinner gets wet, but that the repentant sinner's sins are remitted. Remission is a key term, and it means pardon and forgiveness, as well as the absence of disease or illness.

Biblical baptism is an immersion into the water. Just as you would not bury a corpse with a handful of dirt, you also ought not to baptize a sinner with a couple splashes of water.

1 Peter 3:20 ...when once the longsuffering of God waited in the days of Noah, while the ark was a preparing, wherein few, that is, eight souls were saved by water.

21 The like figure whereunto even baptism doth also now save us (not the putting away of the filth of the flesh, but the answer of a good conscience toward God,) by the resurrection of Jesus Christ:

Water baptism is an essential part of the salvation plan of God. You would not dare to delete the Red Sea crossing from the story of the Exodus, nor would you remove the Brazen Laver from within the Tabernacle. You also would not fail to mention the burial of Jesus Christ whenever you are directing a Passion Play. When I say that water baptism is "essential" what I mean is that if you remove water baptism from the Gospel, it is no longer the Gospel of Jesus Christ. Jesus did not argue with John the Baptist about who really needed to be baptized, but he gently insisted that John fulfill his priestly office:

Matthew 3:15 And Jesus answering said unto him, Suffer it to be so now: for thus it becometh us to fulfil all righteousness. Then he suffered him.

Jesus said it simply and clearly! Baptism is necessary to fulfill all righteousness. I, personally, want to be filled full with the effects of the righteousness of Jesus Christ. I realize that there are individuals and entire denominations who do not hold water baptism in such high regard. In the days of John the Baptist it was no different. Jesus did have something to say about such rebels.

Luke 7:30 But the Pharisees and lawyers rejected the counsel of God against themselves, being not baptized of him.

31 And the Lord said, Whereunto then shall I liken the men of this generation? and to what are they like?

Notice the strong language in this passage. It was "the counsel of God" that they were rejecting. I encourage you to open your Bible and read the answer that Jesus provided to his own rhetorical question. These stubborn men were like petty children who took their toys home and refused to play. They were observers and critics of this thing called the Kingdom of God, but they were not partakers. They were not believers. These religious leaders don't seem to be the least bit interested in a biblical life of faith, unlike another man that Jesus once encountered.

Mark 9:23 Jesus said unto him, If thou canst believe, all things are possible to him that believeth.

24 And straightway the father of the child cried out, and said with tears, Lord, I believe; help thou mine unbelief.

Lord, please help us to receive the Gospel!

Spirit Baptism

The Gospel narrative offers us a glimpse of what John saw when Jesus came up out of the water. He described it this way:

John 1:32 And John bare record, saying, I saw the Spirit descending from heaven like a dove, and it abode upon him.

33 And I knew him not: but he that sent me to baptize with water, the same said unto me, Upon whom thou shalt see the Spirit descending, and remaining on him, the same is he which baptizeth with the Holy Ghost.

Regardless of what some preachers might tell you, Jesus was not himself baptized with the Holy Spirit at this time. This event is clearly an attempt on God's part to communicate a truth. Luke 1:15 tells us that John the Baptist was filled with the Holy Ghost from his mother's womb. How much more certain can we be that the Lord Jesus Christ, who was miraculously conceived in the womb of the Virgin Mary, was complete and at rest in the presence of his father. The Holy Spirit is none other than the Spirit of Christ. (See Romans 8:9 and 1 Peter 1:11) He did not need an infilling any more than he needed the repentance or the washing of water. You and I desperately need it all, and by the grace of God no sincere seeker is ever turned away.

Matthew 11:28 Come unto me, all ye that labour and are heavy laden, and I will give you rest.

29 Take my yoke upon you, and learn of me; for I am meek and lowly in heart: and ye shall find rest unto your souls.

Chapter 11

The Witness of God

---

1 John 5:8 And <u>there are three that bear witness in earth, the Spirit, and the water, and the blood</u>: and these three agree in one.

9 If we receive the witness of men, the witness of God is greater: for <u>this is the witness of God which he hath testified of his Son</u>.

10 He that believeth on the Son of God hath the witness in himself: he that believeth not God hath made him a liar; because he believeth not the record that God gave of his Son.

Proverbs 3:5 <u>Trust in the LORD</u> with all thine heart; and lean not unto thine own understanding.

6 In all thy ways acknowledge him, <u>and he shall direct thy paths</u>.

7 Be not wise in thine own eyes: fear the LORD, and depart from evil.

Most of what we know and believe we learned from other

people. We learn from parents, teachers, preachers, role models, best selling authors, researchers, and heroes. We are surrounded by people who are willing to tell us what they think we should know about anything and everything. Modern media is continually bombarding us with facts and details, much of it intended to influence our buying or voting patterns. To whom should we listen? What can we believe? Who is trustworthy?

The answer is clear! We should believe in God who directs the paths of the righteous. But for many, this is not as simple a matter as it ought to be! You need only compare the teachings of the denominations and it becomes obvious that there are many different doctrinal formulations that force the scriptural language through one interpretive filter or another. We must believe God's word, and God's word alone!

The writers of the Bible employed several methods of placing emphasis on certain passages of particular importance, and the emphasis belongs to God who inspired their writing. One such method is repetition. If the same statement surfaces again and again, you can place a much higher level of importance on the stated principle.

2 Corinthians 13:1 This is the third time I am coming to you. In the mouth of two or three witnesses shall every word be established.

The Spirit, the Water and the Blood happen to be the direct testimony of God himself. This principle pops up in the biblical narrative over, and over on dozens, perhaps hundreds of occasions.

This is the witness of God. This is direct testimony that God has given about his dear Son. If we ever pay attention to anything, we should place a special level of confidence in this three-fold revelation of truth.

Chapter 12

Poured Out at Calvary

John 19:30 When <u>Jesus</u> therefore had received the vinegar, he said, It is finished: and he bowed his head, and <u>gave up the ghost</u>.

34 But one of the soldiers with a spear pierced his side, and <u>forthwith came there out blood and water</u>.

Up to this point we have been tracing the Blood, the Water, and the Spirit throughout the Holy Scriptures. So far, everything has been pointing forward to a single epochal event: Calvary. On a hill called Golgotha Jesus accomplishes his work, and declares "It is finished!" What Jesus does on the Cross spans all of history (Past, Present and Future) and pays the ransom price for all sinners of all times. Old Testament believers spent their days looking forward to the Cross. New Testament believers spend their days looking back to the Cross. John bore witness to what he saw at the Cross with his own eyes. The Cross of Calvary is timeless in its significance and limitless in its scope and power.

A Three-Fold Cord

On the Day of Pentecost Peter sets forth a rationale for the tangible display of Holy Ghost power that is accompanied by the sound of a rushing mighty wind. The people see what is happening, and do not understand what it means.

Acts 2:33 Therefore being by the right hand of God exalted, and having received of the Father the promise of the Holy Ghost, he hath shed forth this, which ye now see and hear.

He hath shed forth this!

Jesus poured himself out, giving us everything that we need for life and salvation. From the Cross of Calvary was poured forth everything that Jesus had to give. He held back nothing!

It is no coincidence that the Bible carefully records the fact that the Spirit, the Water and the Blood were poured out for you and me at Calvary. This is what is required. This is what had always been planned. This is what was promised. And, this is precisely what Jesus accomplished.

This three-fold grace, in direct fulfillment of the word of prophecy, is the witness of God for all to see, and hear, and believe.

Chapter 13

The Passion of Christ

According to the Gospel of Matthew

Matthew 27:50 <u>Jesus</u>, when he had cried again with a loud voice, <u>yielded up the ghost</u>.

59 And <u>when Joseph had taken the body</u>, he wrapped it in a clean linen cloth,

60 <u>And laid it in his own new tomb</u>, which he had hewn out in the rock: and <u>he rolled a great stone to the door</u> of the sepulchre, and departed.

Matthew 28:5 And the angel answered and said unto the women, Fear not ye: for I know that ye seek <u>Jesus, which was crucified</u>.

6 He is not here: for <u>he is risen, as he said</u>. Come, see the place where the Lord lay.

The Gospel recorded by Matthew presents Jesus as Israel's Messiah. Matthew was one of the original twelve disciples who followed Jesus in his earthly ministry, personally witnessing his miracles and sharing in his fellowship with others.

A Three-Fold Cord

Death

This Gospel reveals the fact that, immediately upon the death of Jesus, there was a great earthquake and that the veil in the temple was torn in two from top to bottom. The rending of the veil announced to us that the way to God is now open. The wall of partition that separated man from God has been removed.

Burial

Matthew reports that a man from Arimathaea, named Joseph, begged the Roman Procurator for the right to bury Jesus. He prepared the body, and laid Jesus in his own new tomb, rolling a large stone to block the entrance.

Resurrection

Matthew tells us that the same angel that rolled the stone away from the tomb also announced that Jesus was risen from the dead. The angel sent two women who loved Jesus to tell his disciples that he is risen. Jesus actually met with the women as they were hurrying to the task, and instructed them to tell his disciples that he would meet with them in the region of Galilee. Finally, Matthew chronicles this meeting in Galilee, during which Jesus commissioned the disciples to carry his message to all the nations.

Matthew has faithfully recorded all three of the essential elements of the Gospel: the Death, Burial, and Resurrection of Jesus Christ.

Phillip Stuckemeyer

The Passion of Christ

According to the Gospel of Mark

Mark 15:37 And <u>Jesus</u> cried with a loud voice, and <u>gave up the ghost</u>.

44 <u>And Pilate</u> marvelled if he were already dead...

45 ...he <u>gave the body to Joseph</u>.

46 And he bought fine linen, and took him down, and wrapped him in the linen, and <u>laid him in a sepulchre</u> which was hewn out of a rock, <u>and rolled a stone unto the door</u> of the sepulchre.

Mark 16:5 And entering into the sepulchre, they saw a young man sitting on the right side, clothed in a long white garment...

6 And he saith unto them, Be not affrighted: Ye seek <u>Jesus of Nazareth, which was crucified: he is risen</u>...

The Gospel recorded by Mark presents Jesus as the Christ, the Son of God. John Mark is believed to be the author, and although he was not one of the original twelve disciples, he was a disciple of Simon Peter and probably learned from his teachings.

<u>Death</u>

Mark's Gospel also documents the rending of the veil in the temple immediately upon the death of Jesus.

A Three-Fold Cord

Burial

Mark identifies the man from Arimathaea, named Joseph, as an honorable counselor who waited for the Kingdom of God. When Joseph begged Pontius Pilate for the body of Jesus, Pilate was shocked to hear that Jesus was already dead. The process of crucifixion is brutal, and usually subjects the condemned to many hours of agony. Jesus died quickly because he willingly gave his life to save us. Mark also mentions the fact that Joseph laid Jesus in his own tomb.

Resurrection

Mark details, in a fashion similar to Matthew, the announcement that Jesus was risen from the dead by the angel that rolled the stone away from the tomb. But he further identifies three women who heard the announcement. Mark also records the meeting in Galilee, during which Jesus commissioned the disciples, and adds that the Lord confirmed the preaching of the Gospel with signs and wonders, further authenticating his resurrection.

Mark was equally faithful to include all three essential elements of the Gospel: the Death, Burial, and Resurrection of Jesus Christ.

Phillip Stuckemeyer

The Passion of Christ

According to the Gospel of Luke

Luke 23:46 And when <u>Jesus</u> had cried with a loud voice, he said, Father, into thy hands I commend my spirit: and having said thus, he <u>gave up the ghost</u>.

50 And, behold, there was a man named <u>Joseph</u>...

52 This man went unto Pilate, and <u>begged the body of Jesus</u>.

53 And he took it down, and wrapped it in linen, <u>and laid it in a sepulcher</u>...

Luke 24:6 <u>He is not here, but is risen</u>: remember how he spake unto you when he was yet in Galilee,

7 Saying, <u>The Son of man must</u> be delivered into the hands of sinful men, and <u>be crucified, and the third day rise again</u>.

The author of this Gospel, Luke, was an associate and disciple of the Apostle Paul and also the author of the book of Acts. A physician by trade, Luke was naturally inclined toward careful research, interviews and investigation; however, he wrote under the inspiration of God. Luke also penned The Acts of the Apostles, in which we find the most comprehensive record of the actual preaching of the Gospel of Christ.

A Three-Fold Cord

Luke's record of the Death, Burial, and Resurrection of Jesus is quite similar to the first two Gospels, but he adds a few details.

Death

Luke documents the rending of the veil in the temple immediately upon the death of Jesus.

Burial

Luke notes that Joseph of Arimathaea was not only a counselor, but he was a member of the counsel that condemned Jesus to death. Joseph, however, did not vote in favor of the death penalty. Luke mentions the fact that Joseph laid the body of Jesus in a tomb, but adds that it was a new tomb that had never been defiled with a dead body.

Resurrection

Luke offers a complete record of the angel's announcement that Jesus was risen, but adds that there were yet other women who heard the announcement. There is also a story of Jesus walking and talking with a couple disciples on the road to Emmaus. Finally, Luke provides details of both the great commission and the ascension of Jesus.

As you would expect, Luke's scholarly work recorded all three essential elements of the Gospel: the Death, Burial, and Resurrection of Jesus Christ.

Phillip Stuckemeyer

The Passion of Christ

According to the Gospel of John

John 19:28 When <u>Jesus</u> therefore had received the vinegar, he said, It is finished: and he bowed his head, and <u>gave up the ghost</u>.

41 Now in the place where he was crucified there was a garden; <u>and in the garden a new sepulchre</u>, wherein was never man yet laid.

42 <u>There laid they Jesus</u> therefore because of the Jews' preparation day; for the sepulchre was nigh at hand.

John 20:6 Then cometh Simon Peter following him, and went into the sepulchre, and seeth the linen clothes lie,

9 For as yet they knew not the scripture, that <u>he must rise again from the dead</u>.

John, the Apostle, is known as "The disciple Jesus loved" and also as the writer of the book of Revelation and three epistles. John was an eyewitness of the life, ministry, crucifixion and resurrection life of Jesus. This Gospel emphasizes the divinity of Jesus.

It seems that John was standing closer to the Cross than any of the other disciples, affording him the opportunity to observe what was happening with great detail and accuracy. These were frightful times for the followers of Jesus, who had good reason to fear that they may be taken into custody. John stood by the Cross with Mary, the mother of Jesus, and this Gospel records a conversation that he had with Jesus concerning the care of his mother.

Death

Only the Gospel of John mentions the facts that the Romans broke the legs of the two thieves who were crucified with Jesus in order to hasten their deaths, but that there was no need to break the legs of Jesus since he had already willingly given up the ghost. Instead, a soldier pierced the Lord's side, and John bore witness to the blood and water that poured out of the wound.

Burial

John echo's the other accounts of the burial of Jesus by Joseph, and adds that another ruler of the Jews named Nicodemus assisted in the preparation of the body for burial in a new tomb.

Resurrection

John's account states that both he and Peter ran to the tomb after hearing of the resurrection from the women and that John outran Peter and looked into the tomb first. John also provides specific details about the post-resurrection appearances of Jesus to his disciples.

Section 3

A Timeless Salvation

Ephesians 1:4 According as <u>he hath chosen us in him before the foundation of the world</u>, that we should be holy and without blame before him in love:

9 Having made known unto us the mystery of his will, according to his good pleasure which he hath purposed in himself:

10 <u>That in the dispensation of the fulness of times he might gather together in one all things in Christ</u>, both which are in heaven, and which are on earth; even in him:

11 <u>In whom also we have obtained an inheritance, being predestinated</u> according to the purpose of him who worketh all things after the counsel of his own will:

Chapter 1 discussed the timeless perspective of Almighty God, who sees the end from the beginning. We explored the sovereign plan and purpose of God to salvage a believing remnant, and his clear intention to reveal this plan through his prophets.

Chapter 4 noted that the precious Lamb of God was slain from the foundation of the world, but that is not all God's word says. Let's take special notice of that which the Bible declares has taken place:

Before The Foundation Of The World

- o God's works were finished. (Hebrews 4:3)
- o God's plans were declared to be a secret. (Matthew 13:35)
- o A spotless lamb was slain. (1 Peter 1:19-21, Revelation 13:8)
- o The blood of all the prophets was shed. (Luke 11:50).
- o A holy and blameless remnant was chosen. (Ephesians 1:4)
- o Their names were written in the book of life. (Revelation 17:8)

Before the world that we know was formed, God had decided it all. The deed was done. I literally mean that it was done. Time means nothing to God. Yesterday, today and forever are all the same from Heaven's perspective. And God's plan of salvation is the same in every generation. Never has there been any other way to God than by the Death, Burial, and Resurrection of Jesus Christ.

In the book of beginnings (See Genesis 14:18-20) is found the story of a Priest named Melchizedek who met Abraham as he was returning from a great military victory. This Priest is identified as the King of Salem, and not much other information about the origin or the identity of the man is provided.

Phillip Stuckemeyer

Melchizedek surfaces again in the book of Psalms (See 110:4) in a verse that is prophetically looking forward to Messiah, declaring that he is a priest after the order of Melchizedek. Again, not much other information is provided, but we can put two and two together and this all starts to make sense. Salem means peace, and Jesus is indentified as the Prince of Peace in Isaiah 9:6.

Then, in Hebrews the Apostle Paul begins to shed some light on this matter by emphasizing, in three places (See 5:6, 10 and 6:20) that Jesus is a High Priest after the order of Melchisedec. He then sets out to provide some illumination in the following passages:

Hebrews 7:1 For this Melchisedec, king of Salem, priest of the most high God...

2 ...being by interpretation King of righteousness, and after that also King of Salem, which is, King of peace;

3 Without father, without mother, without descent, having neither beginning of days, nor end of life; but made like unto the Son of God; abideth a priest continually.

These verses clearly identify Jesus as the direct fulfillment of the scriptures, and establish the legitimacy of his Priestly office, which does not find its origin in the Law of Moses.

Hebrews 7:14 For it is evident that our Lord sprang out of Juda; of which tribe Moses spake nothing concerning priesthood.

15 And it is yet far more evident: for that after

the similitude of Melchisedec there ariseth another priest,

16 Who is made, not after the law of a carnal commandment, but after the power of an endless life.

17 For he testifieth, Thou art a priest for ever after the order of Melchisedec.

And this priest is not subject to the same limitations as other priests, since his ministry spans all time, reaching all generations.

Hebrews 7:24 But this man, because he continueth ever, hath an unchangeable priesthood.

25 Wherefore he is able also to save them to the uttermost that come unto God by him, seeing he ever liveth to make intercession for them.

These verses square perfectly with another very familiar passage:

Revelation 1:8 I am Alpha and Omega, the beginning and the ending, saith the Lord, which is, and which was, and which is to come, the Almighty.

From these verses we learn much about the timeless nature of the ministry of the Lord Jesus Christ:

- o He has neither beginning nor ending, in fact he **is** both the beginning and the end of all things – the creator of all.
- o His priesthood predates that established by the Law of Moses, abiding continually, based on his endless life.

- His priesthood continues forever, eternal and unchangeable.
- He has lived and does live and will live forever, and stands in the gap that separates us from a Holy God.
- He can, and always could, save sinners to the uttermost.

And yet, most of us do not live with such an eternal perspective. We could, if we would, but we seem to be locked into a time known as "Now" and in a place known as "Here" and can't seem to think or operate outside of this box known as "My Life."

How can this timeless salvation be presented to a people that lack understanding? How can humans ever fathom such a magnificent grace? How can carnal messengers make it plain? They can't. We can't! This salvation must be preached by the power of the Holy Ghost.

Fortunately, Jesus came to us in the form of a man. God is able to reveal his plans and purposes to us, and through us, with a perspective even we can grasp: **Past, Present and Future.**

Chapter 14

Past, Present and Future

Luke 24:44 ...These are the words which I spake unto you, while I was yet with you, that all things must be fulfilled, which were written in the law of Moses, and in the prophets, and in the psalms, concerning me.

45 Then opened he their understanding, that they might understand the scriptures,

46 And said unto them, <u>Thus it is written, and thus it behooved Christ to suffer, and to rise from the dead the third day</u>:

47 <u>And that repentance and remission of sins should be preached in his name</u> among all nations, beginning at Jerusalem.

48 And ye are witnesses of these things.

49 <u>And, behold, I send the promise of my Father upon you</u>: but tarry ye in the city of Jerusalem, until ye be endued with power from on high.

He opened their understanding, and he transformed their lives. This is what we all need, if there is any hope that we might be saved from sin and serve God with a whole heart.

Romans 1:20 For the invisible things of him from the creation of the world are clearly seen, being understood by the things that are made, even his eternal power and Godhead; so that they are without excuse:

21 Because that, when they knew God, they glorified him not as God, neither were thankful; but became vain in their imaginations, and their foolish heart was darkened.

22 Professing themselves to be wise, they became fools,

Jesus is preparing to commission his disciples and send them on the greatest adventure in the history of mankind. But first, he opens their understanding so that they can fully grasp the wonders of God's salvation plan.

Past

Thus it is written. The scriptures are the foundation, and as Jesus begins to build upon it he makes special mention of the fact that he, himself, is the fulfillment of all things that were written.

Present

Thus it behooved Christ. There is a reason for everything that Jesus has said and done, and everything that has been done to him. There are no accidents, or coincidences. This is God's doing!

Future

Should be preached in his name. It is imperative that we preach God's word God's way. The power of God will accomplish it.

Chapter 15

The Great Commission

According to the Gospel of Luke

Luke 24:47 ...<u>repentance and remission of sins should be preached in his name</u> among all nations, beginning at Jerusalem.

48 And ye are witnesses of these things.

49 And, behold, <u>I send the promise of my Father upon you</u>: but tarry ye in the city of Jerusalem, until ye be endued with power from on high.

God spent the first 4000 years of human history revealing his salvation plan symbolically via the Blood, the Water, and the Spirit. This Three-Fold Cord is intended to point men to the Death, Burial, and Resurrection of Jesus the Messiah, and it only seems reasonable that God's perfect will for the proclamation of the Gospel to the entire world ought to be consistent with this progressive revelation. Also, it would stand to reason that when Jesus commissioned the disciples to spread the Gospel message, he would give explicit instructions to preach all essential elements of this same plan of salvation. We can learn much from his instructions.

Repentance

Even as both John the Baptist and the Lord Jesus charged the people to "Repent" everywhere they went, Luke's record of the great commission shows that Jesus commanded the disciples to preach a message of repentance in his name.

Remission of Sins

John the Baptist also made an essential part of his message the need for baptism in water for the remission of sins. Jesus validates the importance of this part of the Gospel message by commanding the disciples to preach remission of sins in his name. The obvious implication is that the disciples should continue the practice of baptizing in water, and they should do this in his name.

Empowerment of the Spirit

Jesus instructed his disciples to wait for an empowerment before they began their mission. Although the disciples probably did not fully understand what this meant, they would all be baptized in the Holy Spirit within the next couple weeks. What followed immediately thereafter was a demonstration of power that was destined to change the world forever.

The Great Commission was not a challenge to start a new religion. Nor was it a call to another wave of religious and emotional fervor. This was a royal proclamation that would turn the world upside down.

The Great Commission

According to the Gospel of Matthew

Matthew 28:18 And Jesus came... saying, All power is given unto me...

19 <u>Go ye therefore, and teach all nations, baptizing them in the name</u> of the Father, and of the Son, and of the Holy Ghost:

20 Teaching them to observe all things whatsoever I have commanded you: and, lo, <u>I am with you always, even unto the end of the world</u>. Amen.

Philippians 2:9 Wherefore God also hath highly exalted him, and given him <u>a name which is above every name</u>:

10 That <u>at the name of Jesus every knee should bow</u>, of things in heaven, and things in earth, and things under the earth;

In Matthew's account of the Great Commission, Jesus begins by identifying himself as undisputed Lord of all. There is no power or authority in heaven or on earth that is greater than his authority. He is not only Lord of the church; he is also the Lord and judge of all saints and sinners. Therefore, when we go forth as ambassadors who represent the King of Kings, we should pay close attention to the mission and the message to which we have been sent. We will be held accountable!

Making Disciples

The command to "teach all nations" is literally a command to "make disciples" of all the various people groups that inhabit the earth. The making of disciples, by necessity, involves bringing the people under subjection to the word and the will of King Jesus. Those who are openly in rebellion against the righteous rule of their sovereign must be called to a change of mind and a change in direction. This is a call to preach the need for repentance.

Baptizing in the Name

Jesus commands his disciples to baptize the peoples of the earth in a name. This name is the name of the Father, and of the Son, and of the Holy Ghost. Common sense should tell us that Father is a title, not a name. Son is a position, not a name. Holy Ghost is very descriptive, but is not a name. We should pay attention to what the Bible says about this Name that is above all names.

God with us

Jesus declares that he is with us always and forever. Matthew also wrote in Chapter 1 verse 23 that Jesus will be called by the name Emmanuel, which means "God with us." His presence with us and within us is literal and tangible due to the promised infilling of the Holy Spirit, which is an essential element of the Gospel message.

The Great Commission

According to the Gospel of Mark

Mark 16:15 And he said unto them, <u>Go ye into all the world, and preach the gospel to every creature</u>.

16 <u>He that believeth and is baptized shall be saved</u>; but he that believeth not shall be damned.

17 <u>And these signs shall follow them that believe</u>; In my name shall they cast out devils; they shall speak with new tongues;

18 They shall take up serpents; and if they drink any deadly thing, it shall not hurt them; they shall lay hands on the sick, and they shall recover.

Mark's account of the great commission, like Matthew's, repeats the mandate to go into the entire world and preach the Gospel to all people. It is ordinary Christians who are supposed to go. Every believer in King Jesus has been sent to "preach." Some might say "But I am not a preacher," to which I would respond that the act of preaching is a simple act of sharing the hope in a Saviour with another person. You don't need to "preach" in a traditional sense; but you must preach. And when you preach, you do not have the authority to preach whatever you want. Our Lord has given us explicit instructions on what we should proclaim. The sinner must come to God on God's terms:

Believe

Faith is an absolute necessity, but faith in what or whom? Not just any kind of faith will do. You must believe in the Word of God, and in the God who is the word that became flesh. Saving faith is a trust, a reliance, a clinging to Jesus. If you truly see Jesus as he is presented in the Scripture, and if you honestly see yourself as you are (deserving of death and damnation) the only response is to reach out for mercy and grace.

Be Baptized

A true believer will be baptized in water as the scripture has said. The minister of God will compel him to do so. An unbeliever has no confidence in the Word of God, and so even if he does volunteer to get wet, it is not a legitimate burial with Jesus.

Surrender To God's Power To Transform

The working of the Spirit of God in the life of a sinner will always produce results. A biblical conversion is always accompanied by radical change (2 Corinthians 5:17) in the life of the new convert. This is of God, who always confirms his work. A religious convert who fights against the Holy Spirit is no son of God! (Romans 8:14)

It would not be wise to ignore the fact that Jesus made faith and baptism to be matters of salvation and damnation. The preaching of the Gospel is serious business. Eternity is at stake!

The Great Commission

According to the Gospel of John

John 20:21 Then said Jesus to them again, Peace be unto you: <u>as my Father hath sent me, even so send I you</u>.

22 And when he had said this, he breathed on them, and saith unto them, <u>Receive ye the Holy Ghost</u>:

23 <u>Whose soever sins ye remit, they are remitted unto them</u>; and whose soever sins ye retain, they are retained.

John's report of the great commission reads like the account of one who is close to Jesus. The scriptures record that John was "the disciple Jesus loved" and sometimes pictures John as the one who was "leaning on Jesus' bosom." Not only does John record that Jesus spoke "Peace be unto you" but he noticed that Jesus "breathed on them," something that may have gone unnoticed from a distance. This seems to indicate an impartation of the power of the Holy Spirit, not merely a requirement to perform a work of receiving. The recipient of a gift need not put forth the effort. The giver of the gift does the work. There are those modern religionists who present the receiving of the Holy Ghost as work that must be performed as a person earns their salvation. This error must be exposed for the lie that it really is.

Repent

Jesus preached "Repent, for the kingdom of heaven is at hand." (See Matt 4:17) Furthermore, Jesus assured the Jews that he only spoke that which he had learned from his father. (See John 8:28) Jesus was sent to preach repentance. He has also sent us to preach repentance. There can be no doubt about this fact.

Be Baptized

Jesus commissioned the disciples to remit sins. The remission of sins, according to John the Baptist, involves water baptism. We will see later that Peter's first Gospel message will also include baptism for the remission of sins. (See Acts 2:38)

Receive the Holy Ghost

Jesus made it plain that his followers must receive the spirit that he pours out upon them. In Romans 8:9 Paul declares that if any man does not have the spirit of Christ, he does not belong to Christ.

And so it is clear that John has recorded the conversation that Jesus had with his disciples in which he sends them out to deal with the sin problem decisively, once and for all. Not only from his place of authority as King and Judge, but also from his heart as friend and chief lover of men's souls, Jesus sends his messengers of peace on a mission to rescue lost and dying sinners.

Section 4

Future Grace

---

1 John 2:7 <u>Brethren, I write no new commandment unto you, but an old commandment which ye had from the beginning</u>. The old commandment is the word which ye have heard from the beginning.

8 <u>Again, a new commandment I write unto you, which thing is true in him and in you</u>: because the darkness is past, and the true light now shineth.

In Section 1 we considered the ancient types and shadows which were prophetically pointing to the coming of Messiah. The Law, Prophets, and Psalms were all looking forward to Calvary, and as such are examples of bygone grace, extended to us in times past. I say this grace was extended to us, and not only them, because even today we derive the same benefit from the prophetic record that informs, inspires, confirms, and helps us on our pilgrimage.

Section 2 focused on the actual fulfillment of the Old Testament prophetic references to Jesus Christ, specifically detailed in the scriptural and eyewitness accounts

A Three-Fold Cord

of his life and ministry, as well as his crucifixion, death, burial and resurrection. The redemptive works of Jesus on the earth, including his passion and post-resurrection ministry were all examples of the grace that was made manifest in that present day: the day in which the Law of God was fulfilled. We are obviously reaping huge benefits from this grace even today.

In the most recent section, Section 3, the timeless nature of the salvation of God was emphasized. I set forth the principle that the salvation made available to us through the finished work of Jesus Christ on the Cross was also available to the Old Testament saints who were justified by faith in a promised Messiah. In their day the plan of God to save sinners was revealed in a different way, but when they believed God and obeyed the Lord, they were in fact placing their trust in the current manifestation of the salvation of God. Even though the revelation of the Death, Burial, and Resurrection of the Lamb of God was prophetic, often highly symbolic and dramatic, it was a real act of mercy and grace by one whose perspective is timeless. I also addressed the fact that Jesus referred to Past, Present, and Future grace when commanding his disciples to carry the message of the Gospel to all nations. The message is best framed in this time sensitive fashion.

This section, Section 4, is devoted to the future grace that is the object of the daily patience of the Saints as they trust in the promises of God moment by moment, hour by hour and day by day. For us, almost 2000 years later, much of this grace is already past history, yet we still live by faith in future grace, believing the promise of God in every circumstance. We live and overcome temptation by the purifying power that is ours when we hope in God, trusting that he knows what is best for us in all things. As we live our lives in real time, the only grace that matters is future grace; that is, the grace that God will provide one second from now or one hour after that. (I heartily recommend the book "Future Grace" by John Piper of Desiring God Ministries.)

This journey of faith has been the joy of Christian pilgrims ever since the power of God was poured out upon the church on the Day of Pentecost, and the church will continue to triumph by faith until the last day. But has anything really changed substantially since the beginning?

1 John 2:24 Let that therefore abide in you, which ye have heard from the beginning. If that which ye have heard from the beginning shall remain in you, ye also shall continue in the Son, and in the Father.

Wouldn't it be rather presumptuous of us to assume that our joy in Jesus exceeds the joy experienced by Abraham or David? They trusted in God, and were accepted in the beloved. They were moved by the Holy Ghost, and at times were even filled with the Spirit of God. Is there really a significant difference in the grace of God that is our daily allotment, our draw on an eternal inheritance? That is the purpose of this section. By analyzing the message that turned the world upside down, and paying close attention to how the early church accomplished its mission, we will be better able to comprehend the full depth, and breadth, and height, and length of the marvelous grace of God. The covenant that God keeps with his people is the legacy handed down by the Saints that have passed on before us, and the continuing heritage of the Saints that will follow on to know the Lord both with us and after us. (Ephesians 3:17-19)

Past / Present / Future

In the Great Commission, especially as recorded in the book of Luke, Jesus intentionally overlaid the events of redemptive history upon a timeline stretching from eternity past to eternity future. The redeemed were chosen before the foundation of the world, and will rule and reign with Jesus forever, and the present reality of life on this planet only makes sense when founded upon the rock; that is, upon Jesus Christ. A man without God is searching for answers, and the anointed preaching of the Gospel of the Bible resonates within his heart as the Spirit of the Lord draws him. We all know what it is like to wonder "Where did I come from? Why am I here? Where are we going?" The Bible message answers these questions in a most compelling way. It can be difficult for those who hear the Gospel to categorize and compartmentalize the many facts of the Bible, but the work of saving the world is more a matter of truths than of facts. I personally, as a teacher by both gifting and inclination, tend to get bogged down in details. Those to whom I minister can easily be lost in an endless barrage of facts and figures, and may completely miss the whole point. Jesus knows best how to save us!

Jesus was preparing Peter and the other disciples for their world-wide mission. He knew that this work would begin in the Jewish world of teachings and traditions, and that for many of the disciples their entire ministries would be focused on the Jewish community. Presenting the Gospel to a group of hearers who have studied the Holy Scriptures from childhood poses a unique set of challenges, ranging from cultural predisposition to outright religious bias. While preaching to the Jews on the Day of Pentecost, Peter employed the Bible method:

Past – He began by laying a historical foundation. By affirming what was written by the Prophets he defused the tendency to object that can easily short circuit the salvation of a hearer who holds a deeply religious world view.

Present – He proceeded directly to the events that had recently unfolded in the last few weeks and years. Though these events are in the distant past for you and I, they were contemporary events for those who went out to hear Jesus teach, and who were wondering about the recent reports of his resurrection that were the talk of the town in Jerusalem.

Future – Peter answered the question "What shall we do?" and skillfully connected the dots. What the prophets said would come to pass rang true in the life, death, burial, and resurrection of Messiah. And God demands a response from each of us.

History and eschatology (the study of last things) are potent allies to the simple message of the Cross. On the other hand, historical and eschatological fables are enemies of the Cross.

The Ageless Covenant

It is customary for modern believers to speak of the relationship of God and his people in terms of covenants and dispensations. Volumes have been written extolling the virtues of a deity who supposedly is holding all men accountable for the same sin nature, and who consistently points those men to the same savior, but who somehow has decided to offer redemption in vastly different ways based solely on the timing of one's birth. Many critics of the Christian religions think it to be quite absurd that one man, born long ago, had to kill all those calves and sheep to pacify God, while another man born a few millennia later only has to sit on a padded pew and believe a few stories about a distant historical figure, while waiting for the rapture.

In Chapter 7 of this book I expressed my concern that modern doctrinal innovators have seduced millions of churchgoers into taking their eyes off the prize (see Philippians 3:7-15). What distracts them is a hollow promise that God has reserved some mysterious revelation that can only be understood in the end times by a select few who are the beneficiaries of a special covenant.

What the Bible really says about the covenant God made with men should challenge us to think again. I declare here and now that there is no difference in the covenant God made with Moses and the covenant God made with Peter and Paul; or with us.

1 John 2:1 My little children, these things write I unto you, that ye sin not. And if any man sin, we have an advocate with the Father, Jesus Christ the righteous:

2 And he is the propitiation for our sins: and not for ours only, but also for the sins of the whole world.

You may object to my use of this passage of scripture in such a context. You might point out that Jesus hadn't yet been born in the days of the old covenant, much less crucified and resurrected. Plus, you might add, there is that set of Laws that they had to deal with, but that we can almost completely ignore.

1 John 2:3 And hereby we do know that we know him, if we keep his commandments.

4 He that saith, I know him, and keepeth not his commandments, is a liar, and the truth is not in him.

5 But whoso keepeth his word, in him verily is the love of God perfected: hereby know we that we are in him.

6 He that saith he abideth in him ought himself also so to walk, even as he walked.

But wait, screams the modern churchman! You cannot possibly be suggesting that we are required to keep the law in the same way that the members of the tabernacle congregation were, can you? Actually, that is not the point at all. The Bible makes it clear that no man was ever justified by keeping the law. I am suggesting that our feeble understanding of the covenant that God made in days of old is horribly flawed. And, I think, this misunderstanding tends to skew our modern notion of how God deals with us.

A Three-Fold Cord

1 John 2:7 Brethren, I write no new commandment unto you, but an old commandment which ye had from the beginning. The old commandment is the word which ye have heard from the beginning.

You see, there is only one set of commandments. Contrary to popular belief there is not one set of rules for the Old Testament people and a different set of rules (or the absence of rules) for New Testament people. There is only one set of rules, period!

1 John 2:8 Again, a new commandment I write unto you, which thing is true in him and in you: because the darkness is past, and the true light now shineth.

Either there is a new commandment or there is not! Can you have it both ways? It is precisely the carnal Christian who wants it both ways. Many modern scholars also seem to want it both ways. They want the Bible to say one thing to others, and something entirely different to themselves. We tend not to mind if most of the population will be judged by the Law, as long as we are not judged by the Law. It is common for religious people to delight in the rule of law when it is the transgressions of others that are in the spotlight. But when it comes to their own transgressions, they want to believe that Jesus has somehow forgotten that they ever sinned. (Ever heard of a sea of forgetfulness?) One modern notion of grace is that because of my profession of faith God is under some sort of obligation to allow me to enter the kingdom, my lackluster performance at walking out those things that I profess to believe notwithstanding.

Now, I am not a proponent of Legalism. Nor do I

advocate that everyone will eventually be saved (as is true of Universalism or Ultimate Reconciliation). I understand that there is a heaven and a hell. I am a lover of the grace of God, and I delight myself in the God of grace. But grace was never intended to be easy, sleazy, or greasy. Grace is the very nature of a God who takes pity on a people that has been ravaged by the effects of sin, and who has determined within himself to rescue a faithful remnant from the power of sin. We are end time beneficiaries of this gift, but there have been other recipients of this same gift of grace since the earliest days of human experience and history.

Consider the Amplified Bible's rendering of these two passages:

1 John 2:7 Beloved, I am writing you no new commandment, but an old commandment which you have had from the beginning; the old commandment is the message which you have heard [the doctrine of salvation through Christ].

8 Yet I am writing you a new commandment, which is true (is realized) in Him and in you, because the darkness (moral blindness) is clearing away and the true Light (the revelation of God in Christ) is already shining.

There you have it! The new commandment is the same as the old commandment. The difference is that, because of the finished work of Jesus Christ, we now actually have a chance of walking in the new covenant by the power of the Holy Ghost. The darkness is past. The true light shines. We no longer walk in darkness.

And yes, I am aware that the scriptures say the old covenant

A Three-Fold Cord

vanishes away (Hebrews 8:13) but we must understand this in the light of the Cross. Hebrews also has a few other things to say:

Hebrews 8:8 For finding fault with them, he saith, Behold, the days come, saith the Lord, when I will make a new covenant with the house of Israel and with the house of Judah:

9 Not according to the covenant that I made with their fathers in the day when I took them by the hand to lead them out of the land of Egypt; because they continued not in my covenant, and I regarded them not, saith the Lord.

10 For this is the covenant that I will make with the house of Israel after those days, saith the Lord; I will put my laws into their mind, and write them in their hearts...

No perceived failure of the old covenant is a failure of God's word or God's plan; he has always upheld his part of the covenant relationship. The problem has always been that unfaithful men are unwilling or unable to continue in the covenant. This is a failure of sinful men. And the solution is the same solution that God first set forth from the beginning. The innocent must take our place and pay the ultimate price. We go free, and the amazing thing is that we walk free indeed. (John 8:36) This is not a matter of God overlooking our bondage, but is God reaching us in our sin and changing the fundamental condition of our hearts. This is the gift of grace that is available to all.

Continuing In The Covenant

The Bible emphatically declares the faithfulness of God

toward his covenant people. Jesus will spare no expense as he prepares for the bride who is the love of his heart. He bought her back from her captors, and he has no intention of losing her again!

1 Corinthians 1:4 I thank my God always on your behalf, for the grace of God which is given you by Jesus Christ;

5 That in every thing ye are enriched by him, in all utterance, and in all knowledge;

6 Even as the testimony of Christ was confirmed in you:

7 So that ye come behind in no gift; waiting for the coming of our Lord Jesus Christ:

8 Who shall also confirm you unto the end, that ye may be blameless in the day of our Lord Jesus Christ.

9 God is faithful, by whom ye were called unto the fellowship of his Son Jesus Christ our Lord.

The words the King James translators penned as "confirm you" appear in other versions of the Bible as sustain you, keep you, or establish you and from this we understand that God will uphold his part of the covenant unto the end. The Almighty brings his limitless power to bear on behalf of each individual saint. If Jesus chose you, drew you by his Spirit, and redeemed you, he will also complete you. Of this you can be certain!

Philippians 1:6 Being confident of this very thing, that he which hath begun a good work in you will perform it until the day of Jesus Christ:

I am concerned about those reckless church folk who seem to think that the grace of God guarantees a place in heaven for thousands of professors who continue to live like servants of Satan.

Romans 6:1 What shall we say then? Shall we continue in sin, that grace may abound?

2 God forbid. How shall we, that are dead to sin, live any longer therein?

Paul was not expressing a callous disregard for the eternal security of multitudes of the lost and dying. Far from it! Paul was voicing his honest opinion that it is impossible for the saints of God to willingly live a life of sin and degradation. After all, how can a dead man live such a life? We are dead, aren't we?

Colossians 3:2 Set your affection on things above, not on things on the earth.

3 For ye are dead, and your life is hid with Christ in God.

But how does a dead person live at all, much less set his or her affections on things above? The Kingdom of God is an upside down kingdom. If you want to be first, you must be last (Mark 9:35) and if you want to be great, you must become a servant (Mark 10:44). If you humble yourself, the Lord will lift you up (James 4:10) and by faith, the dead live (John 11:25). These truths are firmly rooted in the scripture. However, as equally paradoxical as it may seem, the Bible does not teach that the saints continue in sin. God's word does not say that you will sin a little every day.

Phillip Stuckemeyer

Ephesians 2:8, 9 are favorite verses of those who say that "grace" means "unmerited favor" while insisting that God overlooks willful transgressions and takes us to heaven in spite of them. I wholeheartedly agree that the grace of God is full of favor, and that we do not deserve any of it.

Ephesians 2:8 For by grace are ye saved through faith; and that not of yourselves: it is the gift of God:

9 Not of works, lest any man should boast.

We do not earn our salvation by meritorious works of righteousness. There is no works-based salvation; and yet, there is much work to be done in a believer's life. We are dead, and dead men do not work!

Strong's Concordance defines "grace" this way:

> ...of the merciful kindness by which God, exerting his holy influence upon souls, turns them to Christ, keeps, strengthens, increases them in Christian faith, knowledge, affection, and kindles them to the exercise of the Christian virtues...

This popular Bible study reference has correctly captured the essence of the grace of God. Yes, there is much work that must be accomplished in the saving of a sinner, and it is the Lord Jesus Christ himself who does the work!

Ephesians 2:10 For we are his workmanship, created in Christ Jesus unto good works, which God hath before ordained that we should walk in them.

We are his workmanship, true enough! This verse also says

we were created for good works, and that we should live accordingly. Those who would prefer to remain in their sin will almost always deny this fact, and will often accuse the faithful of legalism.

Hebrews 4:9 There remaineth therefore a rest to the people of God.

10 For he that is entered into his rest, he also hath ceased from his own works, as God did from his.

11 Let us labour therefore to enter into that rest, lest any man fall...

How do we resolve the apparent contradiction? The answer is to be found in the definition of grace. God, the almighty, exerts his mighty power upon our souls and transforms us into overcomers. We continue in the covenant because of the power of the Holy Spirit who dwells in our hearts by the faith of Jesus Christ.

16th Century proponents of sovereign Grace believed in the perseverance of the saints. By this they meant that the Saints of God will be faithful until the end because of the faithfulness of the God of grace. As Strong's Concordance suggests, God's grace offers to us much more than a false hope that God will pretend we have never sinned. Instead, the power of God truly sets us free from the bondage of sin. All that we need to do is to stay with Jesus. If we abide in him, he promises to abide in us, and if Jesus lives his endless life in us, then we are secure in that life forever.

It is imperative that we continue in the covenant that God has made with us through the death, burial, and resurrection of Jesus Christ. Jesus did the work on the Cross, and we are the beneficiaries of this marvelous grace. There is safety near the Cross, and we began our Christian lives with an upward glance at the Savior who offers to be with us through the good times and the bad times. We can trust in God, no matter what tribulations we might face. We must bank our futures on the Messiah. This is non-negotiable.

There are many Bible verses that speak of the conditional nature of God's promises, and of our need to be faithful to the end. I will finish this chapter by quoting a few of them.

Hebrews 3:6 But Christ as a son over his own house; whose house are we, if we hold fast the confidence and the rejoicing of the hope firm unto the end.

Hebrews 3:14 For we are made partakers of Christ, if we hold the beginning of our confidence stedfast unto the end;

Hebrews 6:11 And we desire that every one of you do shew the same diligence to the full assurance of hope unto the end:

Revelation 2:26 And he that overcometh, and keepeth my works unto the end, to him will I give power over the nations:

Chapter 16

The Keys to the Kingdom

Matthew 16:13 When Jesus... asked his disciples, saying, Whom do men say that I the Son of man am?

16 And Simon Peter answered and said, <u>Thou art the Christ, the Son of the living God</u>.

17 ...Blessed art thou, Simon Barjona: for flesh and blood hath not revealed it unto thee, but my Father which is in heaven.

18 And I say also unto thee, That thou art Peter, and <u>upon this rock I will build my church</u>; and the gates of hell shall not prevail against it.

19 <u>And I will give unto thee the keys of the kingdom of heaven</u>: and whatsoever thou shalt bind on earth shall be bound in heaven: and whatsoever thou shalt loose on earth shall be loosed in heaven.

20 Then charged he his disciples that they should tell no man that he was Jesus the Christ.

In this familiar passage of Scripture Jesus gives the keys of the kingdom of heaven to Simon Peter. Keys are used to lock or unlock, or perhaps to restrain or release, something or someone. In this case the context makes it clear that these keys will either be used to loose people who are shackled by the bondage of sin, or to bind evil spirits who would trouble the saints. Furthermore, in the not too distant future Jesus will ascend into the heavens, and it will be Peter's job to preach the Gospel first in Jerusalem. You might say that Peter will be opening a door, granting access to all people who want to gain entry into the Kingdom of God.

In Revelation 3:19-22 Jesus characterizes the barrier between God and man as a door that must be opened by the man. After challenging us to repent, Jesus says that if we open the door he will come in and fellowship with us. He goes on to say that any man who overcomes will be granted a special place with Jesus. He actually states that the overcomer will sit with him in his throne, which could mean a place of authority, judgment, or administration within the kingdom. Apparently there is a natural progression in this eternal dialogue between God and men. There is the opening of a door, followed by the kindling of a relationship, and under the best of circumstances the acknowledgement of a victorious, overcoming life. Not every man who hears the knock on the door will actually open that door. Not every man who meets the Saviour for the first time will go on to develop a committed relationship with the Saviour. Not every man who determines to serve the Lord Jesus will qualify as an overcomer. Not every man who is entrusted with authority will exercise that authority well. It should be no surprise, then, that we are challenged to pay attention to what the Spirit of God is saying to the church.

The desire of all men throughout all ages is to return to the Garden of Eden. Only Adam and Eve enjoyed this special relationship with God. They had direct access to the creator, had been given positions of responsibility, and were unhindered by the sin that drives us away from the presence of God, robbing us of our inheritance. Sin is the door that separates us from God, and might seem like prison bars on one occasion, or like an impenetrable wall on another occasion. Sin deprives us of the joy and satisfaction for which we have yearned since birth. We exhaust ourselves trying to strengthen this door, and in a thousand ways we build this wall brick by brick, and stone by stone. We work overtime to drive God out of our consciousness, but the nagging need for God remains. Jesus could knock the door off its hinges, or he could obliterate the wall of separation, but this suspension of the rule of law would force a people into servitude. Instead, God has mounted a 4,000 year long campaign to solve the sin problem once and for all. Only then can we legitimately return to our original place of favor, while God's righteousness and justice remain intact. We must voluntarily open the door. Jesus gave the keys to Peter, who must now launch a global key distribution initiative together with the other Apostles of the Lamb.

Jesus had just asked the disciples if they could correctly identify who he was. Peter had been granted understanding by revelation from the Father, and so he correctly identified Jesus as the Messiah, the Son of the living God. Jesus immediately declared that this revelation is the very bedrock upon which the church will be built. Then he announced that Peter will play a pivotal role in this building program. This must have been a sobering moment for Simon Peter, who was present when Jesus condemned the scribes and Pharisees for misusing the keys that had been given to previous generations of leaders and ministers of the covenant. The rebuke went like this:

Luke 11:46 And he said, Woe unto you also, ye lawyers! for ye lade men with burdens grievous to be borne, and ye yourselves touch not the burdens with one of your fingers.

Peter must understand that leadership authority can be abused in such a way that the burdens of the people are increased.

Luke 11:47 Woe unto you! for ye build the sepulchres of the prophets, and your fathers killed them.

Peter needs to remember that, while men tend to build cathedrals and encourage hero worship, it is not mere symbolic gestures that God wants. Disciples will be held accountable for real actions.

Luke 11:52 Woe unto you, lawyers! for ye have taken away the key of knowledge: ye entered not in yourselves, and them that were entering in ye hindered.

Peter should exercise caution to ensure that he uses the Keys of the Kingdom to accomplish the will of the King. This is a solemn responsibility, and the burden has fallen on Peter's shoulders.

In the next few chapters we will carefully consider the message that Peter preached on the Day of Pentecost.

A Three-Fold Cord

Jesus has spent a major portion of the last 3 years equipping his disciples to take the Gospel to all the earth. The investment that God has made in this small band of young Hebrew men will reap huge dividends for the kingdom of God, and Jesus is not willing to entrust the future of the kingdom into the hands of just anyone. He has taught Peter, and shown Peter how to exercise real power. He has chastened Peter, but every rebuke has a redemptive purpose. He has opened Peter's understanding, and will soon open the windows of heaven and pour Holy Ghost power upon him. He has given Peter the model for a message that will change the lives of its hearers. How will Peter handle the pressure? We will see.

Peter must first himself be born again, and only after his own conversion (A total transformation – 2 Corinthians 5:17) will Peter actually find the backbone to confront the nation, and the integrity to faithfully represent the King of Kings as an ambassador sent from the throne with a royal pardon for all who will receive it.

Chapter 17

It Is Written

Proclaiming the Historical Basis for the Gospel

Acts 2:25 For David speaketh concerning him, I foreswa the Lord...

27 Because <u>thou wilt not leave my soul in hell, neither wilt thou suffer thine Holy One to see corruption</u>.

29 Men and brethren, let me freely speak unto you of the patriarch David...

30 Therefore being a prophet, and knowing that God had sworn with an oath to him, that of the fruit of his loins, according to the flesh, he would raise up Christ to sit on his throne;

31 <u>He seeing this before spake of the resurrection of Christ</u>, that his soul was not left in hell, neither his flesh did see corruption.

It was the 50th day after Passover, the Feast of Weeks, what is known to the church as the Day of Pentecost. The city of Jerusalem was filled with Jews who had come to keep the feast, many of them having travelled a great distance from remote places. These were devout Jews who

A Three-Fold Cord

were determined to keep the law as best they could, one of the requirements being that they appear in Jerusalem three times each year. Such Jews were inclined to study the holy books, and therefore were familiar with the many prophecies concerning Messiah's coming. They would also have been in town long enough to hear the latest gossip, most notably the story that was being circulated by the Chief Priests who had bribed the guards to say that the body of Jesus had been stolen by his disciples. This lie was being told because the people were familiar with the prophecy that Messiah would be raised up on the third day. (See Hosea 6:2)

The faithful and obedient disciples had remained in Jerusalem and were spending their time praying, and waiting for the promise of the Father. Suddenly the Holy Spirit was poured out upon them, and the power of God was manifested in some very uncommon ways. There had been a great sound like a mighty wind from heaven, and cloven tongues like fire appeared to each of them. There was great rejoicing and worship. They were speaking in tongues that were not their own. These were very strange events by Jerusalem standards.

The Jews who were in the city heard the commotion and rushed into the street to see what was taking place. They were amazed by what they saw and heard, and assumed that the disciples had been drinking too much wine. The disciples were all behaving quite ecstatically, that is true enough. These devout Jews spoke many different languages. They were well educated, and so they all spoke the ceremonial language of the synagogue and the temple; however each also spoke the language of his homeland.

Understandably, they were quite amazed by the fact that such poorly educated disciples of Jesus were declaring the wonderful works of God in their native language, and doing so quite fluently.

It is unlikely that the disciples of Jesus were preaching, as some have suggested. It is Peter who has been given the keys to the kingdom, and it is his responsibility to open the door. Peter will preach the Gospel on this day, and the other disciples will stand with him in a show of unity. It is more likely that the disciples were exuberantly worshiping God, rejoicing and declaring his many wonderful works. Such behavior routinely accompanies the infilling of the Holy Ghost.

Psalm 107:21 Oh that men would praise the LORD for his goodness, and for his wonderful works to the children of men!

22 And let them sacrifice the sacrifices of thanksgiving, and declare his works with rejoicing.

When Peter heard the suggestion that the disciples were drunk, he rose up publicly and began to address the crowd. The other disciples were with him, and all of them formed a unified front with Simon Peter as the spokesman. On the night that Jesus was subjected to a kangaroo court, Peter had been frightened of a little girl. Today, Peter is bold as a lion. In fact, the Lion of the Tribe of Judah has filled Peter with wisdom and power. Jesus had instructed Peter a few weeks earlier, and now Peter is ready to preach the Gospel in accordance with the will of God.

A Three-Fold Cord

It is no coincidence that Peter begins with a few references to the prophets and the Psalms. This is exactly how Jesus had suggested that the message should be substantiated. "Thus it is written" Jesus had said. So this is how Peter begins to explain to the crowd just exactly what is going on.

The prophet Joel had predicted that the day was coming when God would pour out his Spirit upon all flesh. Today, Peter explains, this prophecy (Joel 2:28, 29) has been fulfilled. God has poured out of his vast supply of power upon these 120 disciples, and their wells are overflowing with living water. (See John 7:37-39)

Later, Peter quotes from Psalm 16:10 as he makes the case for the resurrection of the crucified Messiah. In essence, Peter was saying that the Prophets of old had foretold of this day's events, and the devout Jews should not be surprised by these things. What you see and hear (the wind, the tongues, the declarations, and the rejoicing) is only what the Lord God had promised to shed forth, and which is now authoritative evidence that Jesus was who he said he was.

What is most important for our study is the fact that Peter was careful to preach the Gospel message in a manner that was consistent with the instructions he received from Jesus in the Great Commission as recorded in the Gospel according to Luke.

Luke 24:44 ...all things must be fulfilled, which were written in the law of Moses, and in the prophets, and in the psalms, concerning me.

45 Then opened he their understanding...

46 And said unto them, Thus it is written,...

Pointing to fulfilled prophecy is an extremely effective method of laying the foundation for the message of the death, burial and resurrection of Jesus Christ. Some folks think that all of God's other plans fell through, and so Jesus volunteered to go and die for our sins. No! This was not an afterthought, or some sort of contingency plan. The purpose for laying a foundation of the prophetic word is to prove that the death, burial and resurrection of the innocent Lamb of God was the only salvation plan that ever existed. This lends credibility to what may otherwise sound like the ranting of a lunatic.

Peter was no lunatic. The Gospel is no fairy tale. The Gospel is the power of God unto salvation. (See 1 Cor. 1:18 and Rom. 1:16)

Chapter 18

It Behooved Christ

Proclaiming the Death, Burial and Resurrection

Acts 2:23 <u>Him... ye have taken, and by wicked hands have crucified and slain</u>:

24 <u>Whom God hath raised up, having loosed the pains of death</u>: because it was not possible that he should be holden of it.

27 ...thou wilt not leave my soul in hell, neither wilt thou suffer thine Holy One to see corruption.

32 This Jesus hath God raised up, whereof we all are witnesses.

33 Therefore... <u>having received of the Father the promise of the Holy Ghost, he hath shed forth this</u>, which ye now see and hear.

36 Therefore let all the house of Israel know assuredly, that God hath made the same Jesus, whom ye have crucified, both Lord and Christ.

Once Peter has brought the prophetic basis for the coming of Messiah into the forefront of the minds of his audience, he quickly focuses the discussion directly onto Jesus of Nazareth.

Death

Peter did not beat around the bush. "Him…ye have…crucified and slain" was the charge! Even though it was the Chief Priests and the Counselors who petitioned the Roman Procurator for the death penalty, the entire nation is culpable. The fact is, every man, woman and child on the planet is guilty of the brutal slaying of their savior.

Burial

Peter's reference to the scripture "my flesh shall rest" and "neither wilt thou suffer thine Holy One to see corruption." are directly pointing to the burial of Jesus. Peter was not about to neglect to mention the fact that the body of Jesus laid in a tomb.

Resurrection

"Whom God hath raised up, having loosed the pains of death" and "This Jesus hath God raised up" are the capstone of Peter's message. The resurrection makes the death of this man different from all the false Messiahs in Israel's history. The eyewitness testimony is especially potent, given the emphasis that the Law places on such evidence.

Conclusion

Peter sums it all up by asserting that Jesus is not only the

Messiah that was promised, but that he also is the Lord to whom all others must pay homage. This message was delivered by the power of the Holy Spirit. God is stirring the hearts of the hearers.

Chapter 19

Preach In His Name

Proclaiming the Triumph of the Gospel

Acts 2:37 Now when they heard this, they were pricked in their heart, and said unto Peter and to the rest of the apostles, <u>Men and brethren, what shall we do</u>?

38 Then Peter said unto them, <u>Repent, and be baptized every one of you in the name of Jesus Christ for the remission of sins, and ye shall receive the gift of the Holy Ghost</u>.

39 For the promise is unto you, and to your children, and to all that are afar off, even as many as the LORD our God shall call.

40 And with many other words did he testify and exhort, saying, Save your selves from this untoward generation.

41 <u>Then they that gladly received his word were baptized</u>: and the same day there were added unto them about three thousand souls.

A Three-Fold Cord

As Peter was preaching the Gospel for the very first time, the Holy Spirit was lighting the spark of life in the hearts of many in his audience. Acts 2:37 says "they were pricked in their heart" which is a rather old fashioned way of saying "Peter's words pierced their hearts." In this way the Bible indicates that God was sovereignly moving upon them to bring them to a saving faith so that he could give them the gift of repentance. Jesus had made it plain that this was necessary.

John 6:44 No man can come to me, except the Father which hath sent me draw him: and I will raise him up at the last day.

John 6:65 And he said, Therefore said I unto you, that no man can come unto me, except it were given unto him of my Father.

The Spirit of God was gently bringing conviction upon them as Peter boldly charged them with responsibility for the sin that nailed Jesus to the Cross. Our confidence that God is raising up a chosen generation emboldens us to share our faith with strangers as well as friends. We have no idea who will receive our witness, or when. We only know that Jesus is calling out a people, and that if we share the Gospel, it will accomplish the perfect will of God. Isaiah had prophesied long ago of this ministry of sovereign grace:

Isaiah 55:3 Incline your ear, and come unto me: hear, and your soul shall live; and I will make an everlasting covenant with you, even the sure mercies of David.

Isaiah 55:7 Let the wicked forsake his way, and the

unrighteous man his thoughts: and let him return unto the LORD, and he will have mercy upon him; and to our God, for he will abundantly pardon.

Isaiah 55:11 So shall my word be that goeth forth out of my mouth: it shall not return unto me void, but it shall accomplish that which I please, and it shall prosper in the thing whereto I sent it.

Peter's responsibility was to preach the Gospel. It was God's responsibility to draw sinners, and draw them he did. Before the day was over, more than 3,000 souls would be born again unto a new life in Jesus Christ.

When these people realized that they were guilty, their first inclination was to ask "What shall we do?" Had Peter responded to this question as many modern evangelists do today, his answer might have sounded something like this:

- o Just receive Jesus as your personal savior.
- o Simply believe, and you are saved already.
- o Sign this card, and drop it into the plate.
- o Bow your heads, and raise your right hand.
- o Pray this prayer. Repeat after me…
- o Come to our Wednesday evening Bible study.

Now, none of these answers are inherently wrong. In fact, there have probably been thousands or millions of new believers who entered into the kingdom based on an admonition similar to this. However, Peter's answer was succinct and directly to the point. He told them exactly how to appropriate all that God had made available to them through the Death, Burial and Resurrection of the Lamb of God. We can also follow Peter's lead.

Repent

When we repent, confess our sins, and ask God for forgiveness, we are turning our back on the old man of sin, and are turning to the Lord that we might be born again. Truly, we are made partakers of his death. The Bible says:

Galatians 2:20 I am crucified with Christ: nevertheless I live; yet not I, but Christ liveth in me: and the life which I now live in the flesh I live by the faith of the Son of God, who loved me, and gave himself for me.

Not only does God sovereignly draw us, convict us of sin, and light the flame of faith in our hearts, but the faith by which we come to him is not even our faith. It is "the faith of the Son of God." Our part in this transaction is to let the old man die. God's part is to raise the new man to life in Jesus Christ. And between the death and resurrection there is a burial.

Be Baptized

Not only did Peter instruct his hearers to repent, but also to "be baptized in the name of Jesus Christ for the remission of sins" and this admonition was to "every one of you." These are strong words, and full of stark implications about the appropriate response to the Gospel. If this was the only verse in the Bible that seemed to put forward this principle you might be completely justified in setting it aside or even just ignoring it. You might say "We shouldn't base a doctrine on a single verse of scripture" and be absolutely correct in saying it. But throughout this entire book I have shown that every time the Bible presents the plan of God for the salvation of sinners, there is always found a Three-Fold Cord, unbroken and intact. Water baptism is only one of the three strands, but it is one of the three strands nonetheless.

This conclusion is based on the Holy Scriptures that were penned by men who were "moved by the Holy Ghost" as they put God's purposes and plans into writing. And there are many more Bible verses to consider before this book's final chapter. We cannot pick and choose the Bible verses that we want to accept in order to develop our own religion; at least, not if we hope to be saved. Jesus says that every word is important for sustaining life!

Matthew 4:4 But he answered and said, It is written, Man shall not live by bread alone, but by every word that proceedeth out of the mouth of God.

Every word matters and Peter was faithful to proclaim exactly what Jesus told them to preach. Jesus said that "Repentance and remission of sins should be preached in his name" (Luke 24:47) and that is exactly what Peter preached. Water baptism in the name of Jesus Christ is an essential part of the Gospel, offering hope and salvation to all who hear.

Just as Moses was needed to part the Red Sea in which the man of sin perished, and just as Noah was required to build the ark in which the human race was saved, it is

God's plan that a minister of the Gospel should officiate during this holy act of obedience.

The Bible does not tell us what a minister is supposed to say when a new believer is baptized; and yet, most ministers of the Gospel agree that something ought to be said. Some recite Matthew 28:19. Others carefully strive to obey this scripture, and proclaim "the name" that is above every name: Y'shua, Yahshua, or Jesus. Still others declare "I now baptize you in the name of the Father, and of the Son, and of the Holy Ghost; and that name is Jesus!"

For we who are believers, the commandment of God is that we should "be baptized," not that we would baptize ourselves. There is a public element to this step of faith. After having repented of the sin that kills, the new convert presents himself to the minister of God for burial, and makes a public declaration of faith in the Lord Jesus Christ. He is then immersed in the water in the name of Jesus, and the Bible says that his sin is remitted. The new man is then raised up to walk in newness of life. This new life can only be lived by the power of the resurrected Christ.

The Gift of the Holy Ghost

Peter said that "the promise is unto you, and to your children, and to all that are afar off" which brings the truth of this passage of scripture right up to your own generation. It you confess that you are one of those whom the Lord God has called, you should claim the promise of the Holy Ghost. Peter did not say "you might receive the gift of the Holy Ghost." nor did he say "you have the option or the right to receive or not receive the Holy Spirit."

He boldly declared that "You <u>will receive</u> the gift" and so we are standing on solid footing when we suggest, or even insist that it is God's will that you be filled with this spiritual power.

And yet, in many of the denominations that coexist in today's pluralistic world, the notion of a mighty move of God in the life of a normal believer sounds like madness. There is often an implicit acknowledgment that these passages of scripture exist; however, the authorized doctrinal statements rob them of all power.

2 Timothy 3:5 Having a form of godliness, but denying the power thereof: from such turn away.

I remember when I was a teenager and went through a ritual known as "Confirmation" during which I memorized a number of Bible verses, made a public confession of faith, and was granted access to the communion cup. Near the end of the ritual our Pastor laid his hands on me and said "Receive ye the Holy Ghost." I was a sinner back then. Actually, I was a complete heathen. I had not yet been introduced to the Lord Jesus Christ, much less born again. It would be many years later when I would look up in the midst of a moment of crises, and the many Bible verses that I learned during childhood would produce the fruit for which our Pastors planted the seed of the Word of God in hope of a harvest. The harvest was bountiful

A Three-Fold Cord

in 1978, and I am certain that the Lord of the Harvest is still sending the rain today.

Conclusion

Peter preached repentance, water baptism in the name of Jesus, and the infilling of the mighty Holy Ghost. This was the gold standard for the preaching of the Gospel in his day. It should be no different today. However, I do not want to leave you with the notion that this is some magical formula that guarantees admission into the kingdom of God. Rather, this is how a sinner begins his walk with God. And even Peter acknowledged this fact, for "with many other words" he exhorted the people. It is possible that Peter preached for hours. Yet only a few verses were recorded in the Book of Acts. Surely, these are the most important words.

Chapter 20

The Testimony of Peter

Acts 3:13 The God of Abraham, and of Isaac, and of Jacob, the God of our fathers, hath glorified his Son Jesus; whom ye delivered up...

14 <u>But ye denied the Holy One</u>...

15 <u>And killed the Prince of life, whom God hath raised from the dead</u>; whereof we are witnesses.

16 And his name <u>through faith in his name</u> hath made this man strong...

17 And now, brethren, I wot that through ignorance ye did it, as did also your rulers.

18 But those things, which God before had shewed by the mouth of all his prophets, that Christ should suffer, he hath so fulfilled.

19 <u>Repent ye therefore, and be converted, that your sins may be blotted out, when the times of refreshing shall come from the presence of the Lord</u>.

Lest any who read this book mistakenly assume that Peter's message on the Day of Pentecost has little bearing on modern preaching methods, let us now consider the rest of the Book of Acts. The Gospels gave us detailed accounts of the life, ministry, crucifixion, burial, and resurrection of Jesus, as well as specific instructions for the evangelism of the world. The book of Acts gives us a detailed record of actions the disciples took in direct obedience to the word of the Lord, fulfilling the Great Commission and turning the world upside down. We have already discussed the outpouring of the Holy Spirit upon believers in what some herald as the birth of the Church, but the Book of Acts contains many other records of the works of specific Apostles under a variety of circumstances. The Book of Acts is the most complete history of the proclamation of the Gospel in the entire Bible, and it is no accident that God inspired the writers to record these specific events.

Acts Chapter 3 provides us with insight into a spontaneous occurrence in Jerusalem that drew the attention of a crowd of people who were visiting the temple mount. A man who had been disabled since birth had been carried to a particular temple entrance where he could beg passersby for spare change. This man was a familiar and highly visible reminder that there were still many unfortunate sick and crippled people in the land, in spite of the fact that Jesus healed practically all that he ever encountered. Jesus had also announced that believers would perform greater works than his (See John 14:12), which is amazing when you consider the many miracles that authenticated the ministry of the Son of God.

The events that transpired on the Day of Pentecost had certainly set the grape vine on fire, and would have heightened the expectations of the general population.

This crippled man had not been healed by Jesus during his several passes through Jerusalem. His friends or family members carried him to the Gate called Beautiful each day, but evidently they had never thought to carry him to one of the preaching points where Jesus was healing the sick and maimed. One can only wonder if this fellow, like the blind man in John Chapter 9, was strategically located in this place and at this time for the sole purpose of showing forth the grace and the mighty power that is available in the name of Jesus Christ. It is also quite possible that the Apostles had not yet fully come to grips with the incredible power that Jesus has placed at the disposal of all who trust in him. This event may have been orchestrated by the Holy Ghost to announce to all Jerusalem that the mantle of authority had been transferred from the powerless temple bureaucrats and onto the shoulders of this small band of believers in Messiah.

When this fellow asked for a cash donation that might ease his suffering for a few days, Peter acted in a manner that would change the man's life forever. You may, as I do, harbor a deep mistrust of so called "faith healers" who rent television air time so that they can kick the crutches out from under a seemingly endless stream of crippled people who can never provide any real evidence to support their claims of miraculous restoration. We can't help but wonder where such charlatans come from, much less who sends them the money they need to stay in business!

Peter was the real thing. I'm not sure how it happened. How did the Holy Spirit reveal to him what was about to take place? Did Peter hear a voice, or feel a force moving him? Had Peter been looking for a test case that could be

A Three-Fold Cord

used to experiment with the power that Jesus had promised to unleash? We will never know how it works unless we step out in faith ourselves and believe God. What we do know is that Peter grabbed the man's hand and pulled him to his feet. This man had never been able to stand or walk, but suddenly, supernaturally the strength came into both bone and muscle and he was restored. With much fanfare this man entered into the temple and all present were eyewitnesses of a miracle.

Peter immediately seized upon the opportunity to preach to this group of onlookers. As you would expect, Peter began with a reference to the Old Testament promises of a son who would save the world. He once again accuses the crowd of complicity in the illegitimate arrest and lynching of Jesus. He preached:

Death, Burial and Resurrection

Acts 3:14 But ye denied the Holy One and the Just, and desired a murderer to be granted unto you;

15 And killed the Prince of life, whom God hath raised from the dead; whereof we are witnesses.

The Power of the Name of Jesus Christ

Acts 3:16 And his name through faith in his name hath made this man strong, whom ye see and know: yea, the faith which is by him hath given him this perfect soundness in the presence of you all.

Repentance, Remission of Sins, and Spiritual Renewal

Acts 3:19 Repent ye therefore, and be converted,

that your sins may be blotted out, when the times of refreshing shall come from the presence of the Lord.

It's all there! Peter did not neglect a single point that his master had sent him to preach to the people. This "blotting out of sins" is a theme found in Psalm 51, a passage that would have been very familiar to his listeners! It is no wonder that his preaching produced such grand results. It is also little wonder why what passes for preaching today seems to be so ineffective and weak

The Book of Acts has several other accounts of the preaching of the Gospel for us to consider. Please come with me as we see that the God of the Bible is committed to a complete and consistent presentation of the essential elements of the salvation plan. You, of course, retain the right to decide what you will do with the Word of God. The preaching of the Gospel of Jesus Christ has always, and will always, change the world.

Chapter 21
The Testimony of Philip

Acts 8:34 And the eunuch answered Philip, and said, I pray thee, of whom speaketh the prophet this? ...

35 Then <u>Philip</u> opened his mouth, and began at the same scripture, and <u>preached unto him Jesus</u>.

36 ...they came unto a certain water: and the eunuch said, <u>See, here is water; what doth hinder me to be baptized</u>?

37 And Philip said, <u>If thou believest with all thine heart, thou mayest</u>. And he answered and said, I believe that Jesus Christ is the Son of God.

38 ...and they went down both into the water... and he baptized him.

39 <u>And when they were come up out of the water, the Spirit of the Lord caught away Philip, that the eunuch saw him no more: and he went on his way rejoicing</u>.

When the persecution began in Jerusalem, many believers fled to other cities and countries, preaching the Gospel as they went. This is another example of the sovereign will of God. Philip had been appointed to the office of a Deacon, and had served the body of Christ well. As he grew in grace and in the knowledge of Jesus, Philip was readied for a more substantial role in ministry. Philip went to Samaria and began to preach. The scriptures record the nature and the result of Philip's outreach.

Acts 8:12 But when they believed Philip preaching the things concerning the kingdom of God, and the name of Jesus Christ, they were baptized, both men and women.

13 Then Simon himself believed also: and when he was baptized, he continued with Philip, and wondered, beholding the miracles and signs which were done.

14 Now when the apostles which were at Jerusalem heard that Samaria had received the Word of God, they sent unto them Peter and John:

15 Who, when they were come down, prayed for them, that they might receive the Holy Ghost:

16 (For as yet he was fallen upon none of them: only they were baptized in the name of the Lord Jesus.)

17 Then laid they their hands on them, and they received the Holy Ghost.

The same persecution that was intended to stamp out the threat of this new sect of Jewish believers in Jesus actually served to fan the flames of evangelism. When confronted with displays of hatred and violence, the followers of Jesus found it necessary to trust in God with even greater fervency. God was faithful to provide for their needs, and

A Three-Fold Cord

to pave their way with gladness and joy. They preached Christ with conviction and with enthusiasm.

The Samaritans were despised by the Jews, being considered corrupt half-breeds who were the result of intermarriage between ancient Hebrews and the pagan nations that surrounded them. The grace of God is available to everyone, but it is Peter who has been entrusted with the keys to the kingdom. As you read Acts 8:12-17 it is evident that Philip preached the Gospel. The Samaritans believed in Jesus because Philip preached the death, burial and resurrection. It is reasonable to believe that the message included the call to repentance – Jesus always tied repentance together with his assertion that the Kingdom of God was coming. It is clear that Philip instructed his new converts to be baptized in water in the name of Jesus. Philip also preached the baptism of the Holy Ghost; however, it was necessary for Peter to come from Jerusalem that they might be filled with the Spirit. Peter used the keys to formally open the Kingdom to the Samaritans. (See Acts 1:8)

Eventually, the Lord told Philip to travel South toward Gaza. As he went God gave him an opportunity to minister to an Ethiopian dignitary who was having difficulty understanding a prophecy of Isaiah that concerned the death of the Messiah. Philip began to preach Jesus.

Acts 8:35 Then Philip opened his mouth, and began at the same scripture, and preached unto him Jesus.

It is also clear that this presentation of the Gospel included repentance and water baptism.

Acts 8:36 And as they went on their way, they came unto a certain water: and the eunuch said, See, here is water; what doth hinder me to be baptized?

Philip certainly is not willing to just baptize anyone, so he took the time to inquire about the Ethiopian's faith. Philip wanted to be sure that the man had truly repented and placed his trust in Jesus. There is nothing to be gained by baptizing the man if he has not come to saving faith. Remember, you don't bury someone who is not dead. By repentance we are crucified with Christ. In water baptism, according to the Bible, we are buried with Jesus into his death. (See Romans 6:4) No death, no burial.

Philip was satisfied with the Ethiopian's answer.

Acts 8:37 And Philip said, If thou believest with all thine heart, thou mayest. And he answered and said, I believe that Jesus Christ is the Son of God.

What could Philip possibly want to ensure that the Ethiopian believed, if not in the finished work of Jesus on the Cross? The Ethiopian believed that Jesus was the Son of God because Philip had once again done a good job of presenting the Gospel. It seems obvious that after they considered the Old Testament prophecies he preached the death, burial and resurrection.

Acts 8:38 ...and they went down both into the water... and he baptized him.

The Spirit of God was present in the water to accomplish the work of grace in response to the Ethiopian's faith. When they came up out of the water a miracle occurred.

Acts 8:39 And when they were come up out of the water, the Spirit of the Lord caught away Philip, that the eunuch saw him no more: and he went on his way rejoicing.

40 But Philip was found at Azotus...

The Ethiopian was rejoicing because in the presence of God there is fullness of joy. (See Psalm 16:11) Philip moved on to preach the Gospel to another audience in another city.

Chapter 22

Peter Defends His Testimony

Acts 11:12 And <u>the Spirit bade me go with them</u>... and we entered into the man's house:

13 And he ...had seen an angel... which stood and said unto him, Send men to Joppa, and call for Simon, whose surname is Peter;

14 Who shall tell thee words, whereby thou... shall be saved.

15 And <u>as I began to speak, the Holy Ghost fell on them</u>, as on us...

16 Then remembered I the word of the Lord, how that he said, <u>John indeed baptized with water; but ye shall be baptized with the Holy Ghost</u>.

17 Forasmuch then as <u>God gave them the like gift as he did unto us</u>, who believed on the Lord Jesus Christ; what was I, that I could withstand God?

Simon Peter was a Jew. Centuries of institutionalized mistrust of the nations of the world, together with religious traditions that declare the homes and foods of the

A Three-Fold Cord

Gentiles to be unclean, had fostered a cultural bias that is so deeply ingrained in the fabric of Jewish society that it is hard for even the new Christians to shake. Peter was there when Jesus offered his critique of the tradition that dominated the Jewish religious attitude.

Matthew 15:6 ...Thus have ye made the commandment of God of none effect by your tradition.

7 Ye hypocrites, well did Esaias prophesy of you, saying,

8 This people draweth nigh unto me with their mouth, and honoureth me with their lips; but their heart is far from me.

9 But in vain they do worship me, teaching for doctrines the commandments of men.

In spite of the deep bias that was cultivated in the minds of young Jewish students of the Law, there is nothing inherently unclean about the many meats that were prohibited by the law. Though it may be argued that certain foods are healthier than others (I try to avoid pork, for instance.) God had declared them all good at the creation. Let's consider a few facts:

1. God declared that the whole creation was good.
2. Man was originally designed for a vegetarian diet.
3. After the great flood, God announced that everything was now good for food. This may help to explain the dramatic shortening of the average human lifespan that followed.
4. Moses delivered the Law of God, and thus prohibited many foods.

5. Jesus declared that it is not that which goes into the man that defiles him; rather, it is what comes out of the man.
6. After Calvary, New Testament writers taught that the Law has been fulfilled in Christ, and so the purpose for which certain foods were declared unclean has run its course, and therefore it is acceptable for Christians to eat all of the meats, if they are received with thanksgiving.

The period of time during which the Hebrew's Law prohibited the eating of certain meats is merely a parenthesis within a larger narrative of God redeeming a people from the consequences of sin. In Leviticus Chapter 11 the purpose for the legal prohibitions was revealed. "To separate the clean from the unclean" is how the Bible phrases the purpose for these laws. However, as was pointed out earlier, it cannot be argued that the meats themselves are inherently unclean, so there must be some other meaning. The correct understanding of this passage is that God is separating His chosen people (Israel) from the other nations (Gentiles) for the purpose of protecting a bloodline so that the promised seed could bring forth the Messiah. God is declaring that forced separation will help keep Israel "Clean" compared to the "Unclean" heathen nations. The religious taboos that dominate Judaism make it very difficult for the infant Church to carry the Gospel to the heathen lands. It is time for Peter to use the keys to open the Kingdom of God to the nations.

Peter was quite content to allow the gentiles to perish, in spite of the fact that Jesus had commissioned the church to take the Gospel to all nations. This is a primary reason

A Three-Fold Cord

that God allowed the young church to be persecuted; otherwise they probably would have remained in Jerusalem. When Philip carried the Gospel truth to Samaria, Peter and John came down to pray for the Samaritans so that they might receive the Holy Ghost. After all, though the Jews despised the Samaritans, they were distant relatives. When Philip encountered the Ethiopian ruler and preached the Gospel to him, this was a natural progression for the Church since the Ethiopian was a devoted student of the Hebrew Scriptures, and was most likely a convert to the Jewish religion as the Law allowed.

Now, it is time for Peter to use the keys to grant access to the hoards of Gentile sinners. This does not come easy for Peter, so the Lord goes to great lengths to open Peter's understanding. As Peter reclines on the rooftop of a friend, probably meditating on the promises of God, the Lord challenges his religious sensibilities with a provocative dream that came to him at dinner time.

Acts 10:10 And he became very hungry, and would have eaten: but while they made ready, he fell into a trance,

11 And saw heaven opened, and a certain vessel descending upon him, as it had been a great sheet knit at the four corners, and let down to the earth:

12 Wherein were all manner of fourfooted beasts of the earth, and wild beasts, and creeping things, and fowls of the air.

13 And there came a voice to him, Rise, Peter; kill, and eat.

14 But Peter said, Not so, Lord; for I have never eaten any thing that is common or unclean.

15 And the voice spake unto him again the second time, What God hath cleansed, that call not thou common.

16 This was done thrice: and the vessel was received up again into heaven.

Peter seems quite proud of his confession that he has kept the Law from his youth. Even today, cultural and religious pride tend to short circuit the plan of God in our lives, allowing us to pretend that we are justified when in fact we are only rebelling against the will of God that we should share the good news with the people around us. We reason that "Those people" will never receive us, when in fact it is the Lord Jesus that they need to receive, and if we will just preach the Gospel as we have been commanded, the Holy Spirit will accomplish the work.

Peter doesn't seem to get the point until the Lord emphasizes the simple truth three times, but now he is ready to obey the voice of the Lord. Peter follows the Lord's leading and finds himself preaching the Gospel in the home of one of the hated Romans. It is quite likely that Peter had rather low expectations for this encounter, and that he was shocked when the Lord interrupted his preaching by spontaneously pouring out the Holy Ghost upon this small band of new believers. What was Peter to do? While he was preaching the death, burial, and resurrection and was beginning to transition into a discussion of faith, and repentance, and remission of sins, God dramatically put his stamp of approval on this Gentile expansion of the Kingdom. Peter really had no choice but to welcome these new children of God into the family, and so he boldly commanded them to be baptized in the name of

Jesus Christ. He correctly reasoned that no man could legitimately prohibit these new converts from the waters of baptism, but his associates in Jerusalem may not agree.

When Peter returned to Jerusalem he was called on the carpet and forced to explain why he had paid a visit to the hated Romans who were considered unclean. He rehearsed the entire story, and then reinforced his conclusion with a reference back to the progressive revelation of God's salvation plan.

Acts 11:15 And as I began to speak, the Holy Ghost fell on them, as on us at the beginning.

16 Then remembered I the word of the Lord, how that he said, John indeed baptized with water; but ye shall be baptized with the Holy Ghost.

17 Forasmuch then as God gave them the like gift as he did unto us, who believed on the Lord Jesus Christ; what was I, that I could withstand God?

18 When they heard these things, they held their peace, and glorified God, saying, Then hath God also to the Gentiles granted repentance unto life.

Now the doors are wide open, and the Church is free to carry the Gospel to all the nations. Peter has used the keys of the kingdom effectively, and the world will never be the same. Before we leave this chapter behind, it will be helpful to summarize as follows:

1. Peter preached the simple message of the Gospel. The Three-Fold Cord that is woven throughout the entire biblical narrative includes blood, water, and spirit which point to the death, burial, and

resurrection of Jesus and ultimately prompt our repentance, baptism in water in the name of the Lord, and infilling with God's Holy Spirit.
2. The new Roman believers heard the Gospel, just like every other believer, mixed it with faith, and responded. The appropriate response is always repentance and confession.
3. God authenticated the conversion of these Romans by baptizing them with the Holy Ghost. Sometimes a person's conversion doesn't follow the exact path to God that we think is normal or typical. Here is one such case.
4. Peter recognized that they had been filled with the Holy Spirit because "the Holy Ghost fell on them, as on us at the beginning." Again, he testified "God gave them the like gift as he did unto us," and in this way he signifies that he heard them speak with tongues in the same manner as at the initial outpouring on the day of Pentecost.
5. Finally, Peter determined that these new believers needed to be baptized in water, but he did not merely admonish or encourage them to be baptized, which is customary among preachers. Instead, he assumed the authority that is rightly his, and he "commanded" these new kingdom subjects to be baptized in the name of their King.

Amen! Let it be so! My primary mission in the writing of this book is to show that this is the way the Gospel ought to be proclaimed in all places and at all times. This is God's plan!

Chapter 23

The Testimony of Paul

Acts 19:1 And it came to pass... Paul... came to Ephesus: and finding certain disciples,

2 He said unto them, <u>Have ye received the Holy Ghost since ye believed</u>? And they said unto him, We have not so much as heard whether there be any Holy Ghost.

3 And he said unto them, <u>Unto what then were ye baptized</u>? And they said, Unto John's baptism.

4 Then said Paul, <u>John verily baptized with the baptism of repentance</u>, saying unto the people, that they should <u>believe... on Christ Jesus</u>.

5 When they heard this, <u>they were baptized in the name of the Lord Jesus</u>.

6 And when Paul had laid his hands upon them, <u>the Holy Ghost came on them</u>; and they spake with tongues, and prophesied.

Peter opened the doors wide for the nations of the world to hear the Gospel of Jesus Christ, but it was the Apostle

Paul who was raised up to actually carry the message to the four corners of the earth. Not one of the original twelve disciples, Paul was actually one of the most aggressive persecutors of the early church. This changed dramatically after an encounter with Jesus on the road to Damascus. Paul was chosen of God for a very distinctive ministry.

God spoke to Ananias, one of his servants in Damascus, and sent him to Paul. Ananias objected, having heard of the man's evil reputation. Luke records this dialogue:

Acts 9:15 But the Lord said unto him, Go thy way: for he is a chosen vessel unto me, to bear my name before the Gentiles, and kings, and the children of Israel:

16 For I will shew him how great things he must suffer for my name's sake.

Later, Paul is telling the story in his own words.

Acts 22:14 And he said, The God of our fathers hath chosen thee, that thou shouldest know his will, and see that Just One, and shouldest hear the voice of his mouth.

15 For thou shalt be his witness unto all men of what thou hast seen and heard.

16 And now why tarriest thou? arise, and be baptized, and wash away thy sins, calling on the name of the Lord.

Here are a few observations about Paul's conversion experience:

A Three-Fold Cord

1. God had sovereignly chosen Paul.
2. Paul saw the resurrected, glorified Jesus with his own eyes.
3. Paul was struck blind by the sight and sat in darkness. Stunned by the reality of it all, he did not eat or drink for 3 days. Imagine how much repenting was going on. Paul was responsible for the arrest and death of many believers.
4. A minister of God came to him to confirm the Lord's good intentions, and commanded him to be baptized.
5. Ananias actually told Paul that in water baptism his sins would be washed away, calling on the name of the Lord.
6. When he came up out of the water his sight was restored, and as part of the package he was also filled with the Holy Spirit. (See Acts 9:17)
7. Paul then went into Arabia and spent no small amount of time seeking after God and receiving his Gospel by revelation directly from the Lord. (See Galatians 1:15-18)

As is true with all of us, Paul's conversion experience shaped his idea of what should be the normal Christian experience. This would also have a profound impact on the nature of his ministry. Paul was a Hebrew of the Hebrews, having studied at the feet of some of the most eminent scholars. When Paul entered a city, it was his custom to seek out the Jews who met in a local synagogue, and to share with them his personal testimony. Whenever the Jews rejected the message of the Cross (which they normally did) then Paul would take the Gospel to the

Gentiles. Paul hoped for the best whenever he encountered someone who professed faith in the God of the Bible, and usually gave them the benefit of the doubt until they proved that they were unworthy. We can learn a lot from Paul, and particularly from the way that he interacted with people of faith. We live in a pluralistic society, and often cross paths with people who tell us they are God's people. How would Paul respond? Our study takes us to Acts Chapter 19.

Acts 19:1 And it came to pass, that, while Apollos was at Corinth, Paul having passed through the upper coasts came to Ephesus: and finding certain disciples,

Paul had stumbled upon a group of people who were zealous for Messiah. Evidently, he joined them for fellowship. He was not sure who they were or what they believed, but he seems to have assumed that they were genuine believers. And, in fact, they were genuine in their faith. They were just not at the same level as Paul.

We often run into people who tell us they are Christians, or members of a church, or students of the Bible, or disciples of the Lord Jesus. One of the most offensive character traits that accompany spiritual pride is the arrogant assumption that everyone else is spiritually inferior to oneself. You have met these types of folks, haven't you? They are immature and fully deserve the insult that many sinners rely on when they want to criticize the church: Holier Than Thou. Unfortunately, our critics probably have met several of this type of people, and tend to assume that we are all just like them. So, how should we respond

A Three-Fold Cord

to strangers who represent themselves as the children of God? We should:

- o Entreat them as the Children of God that they claim to be, and look for ways to encourage them in their walk of faith.
- o Engage them in conversation, being sensitive to the leading of the Holy Spirit. You do not want to drive them away.
- o Understand that they probably began their pilgrimage in a different place than where you began, and they have most certainly followed a different path. At any rate, they have arrived at this place and at this time, and you may have a chance to help them along on the way to God.
- o Carefully assess where they stand with God. Perhaps you can minister to them. Just maybe they will minister to you.
- o Maintain a peaceable attitude, and let Jesus direct the course that you follow as the relationship takes shape.

Acts 19:2 He said unto them, Have ye received the Holy Ghost since ye believed? And they said unto him, We have not so much as heard whether there be any Holy Ghost.

Paul asks probing questions. Notice that he crafts this question in such a way as to acknowledge the genuineness of their faith. He really is trying to find out if the whole Gospel has been preached to them, and if they have profited from the Gospel truth. There is a good chance that during the earlier conversation Paul has heard a few things that do not ring true. It is likely that the Holy Ghost that resides within Paul has alerted him to the fact that something is wrong. He must find out how far they have progressed in Christ, or where their growth and development have been arrested.

The disciples honestly tell Paul that they are ignorant of these things. They have not even heard of the Holy Ghost. This is very important. Often times you may encounter people who are not honest about where they stand or what they have experienced in God. It can be very difficult to discern the facts, and so it is imperative that you pay attention to the leading of the Spirit.

Acts 19:3 And he said unto them, Unto what then were ye baptized? And they said, Unto John's baptism.

Now Paul realizes where these disciples stand, and he can proceed to share with them the rest of the Gospel. Paul knows that the Three-Fold Cord cannot be broken, and he is aware that the normal Christian experience usually includes certain key milestones on the way to an overcoming life of faith by grace.

1. The sinner is chosen by God's grace. The Bible says that this occurred before the foundation of the world.
2. The Holy Spirit begins to draw the sinner, lighting the spark of life. They cannot come unless they are drawn!
3. God sovereignly orchestrates an encounter with a minister of the Gospel. There may be multiple encounters with believers throughout a person's

A Three-Fold Cord

life, and each time an important puzzle piece may be put into place.

4. The essential elements of the Gospel are shared with the sinner by these witnesses, some more skillful than others. We sow the seed; God gives the increase!

5. The Holy Spirit convicts the person of sin, and this awareness of sin brings them to the moment of decision.

6. The sinner mixes the Word of God with faith. This faith is another gift of a loving God who saves all whom he calls.

7. Moved by the Spirit within, the sinner lifts up his eyes to a Holy God, confesses his sins, asks for forgiveness, and relinquishes control of his own life in the hope of salvation. This is a death – the debt was paid on the Cross by Jesus.

8. God hears the prayer of faith, and accepts the sinner into the beloved family known as "The Church," which is also the body of Christ. This is "The new birth" and in this way the sinner is born again unto a new life in Christ. The old way is history. Everything changes by faith through grace.

9. The new child of God is buried by water baptism into the death of Christ by a minister of the Gospel. This baptism is "in the name of Jesus Christ" in much the same way that everything a believer does ought to be from the heart and in the name of the Lord.

10. God fills the new saint with resurrection life. In this way the new convert is raised from the dead

by the same spirit that raised Jesus from the dead. This truth is prefigured by the bringing forth of the new believer from the waters of baptism. This often involves the direct involvement of a minister of the Gospel through the laying on of hands. The laying on of hands is very similar to the actions that a doctor or nurse takes in a maternity ward to encourage a newborn baby to take that first breath of life. There is a certain sound announcing that all is well.

11. The new member of the body of Christ grows in grace and in the knowledge of Jesus. Such growth takes time, as well as the intervention of those ministers of the Lord who have been entrusted with the care and feeding of the new convert. This process involves teaching, and the systematic discovery of the person's gifts and calling. They take their place in the body of Christ and begin to contribute to the body life.

12. The saint of God matures and serves, and perseveres unto the end of life, however long or short that may be, by faith.

Again, the actual experience of an individual believer will be unique, but will usually include these key milestones. Each case is different, but the Word of God sets forth the standard.

Now that Paul understands that these are disciples of John, he is better able to minister to them. He began with the assumption that they had been filled with the Holy Ghost, and when he discovered that this was not the case,

A Three-Fold Cord

he worked his way back one step at a time as necessary to ascertain where their growth had stagnated.

Acts 19:4 Then said Paul, John verily baptized with the baptism of repentance, saying unto the people, that they should believe on him which should come after him, that is, on Christ Jesus.

5 When they heard this, they were baptized in the name of the Lord Jesus.

6 And when Paul had laid his hands upon them, the Holy Ghost came on them; and they spake with tongues, and prophesied.

They were true believers, but they had only heard the Gospel preached from the perspective of John the Baptist. It is possible that they had never even met John the Baptist, but may have responded to the ministry of one of John's disciples. This is an amazing thing as far as I am concerned. John the Baptist had encouraged his disciples to follow after Jesus. How an entire branch of the Church of John the Baptist had developed with no knowledge of the death, burial and resurrection of Jesus remains a mystery to me. You will encounter all sorts of situations.

You will meet people who were raised as Catholic, Lutheran, Episcopalian, Baptist, Methodist, Disciples of Christ, Pentecostal, Charismatic, Fundamentalist, Liberal, Legalist, Socialist, Mormon, Jehovah's Witness, Scientologist, and who knows what else. They all will have a different testimony, a different experience, and a different outlook. Almost all of them will believe that their own faith is the truly orthodox faith. Some of them will have met Jesus.

Phillip Stuckemeyer

I myself was raised as a Missouri Synod Lutheran. My parents encouraged me to pray daily. We gave thanks before our family meals. We were regular church attenders. My parents gave financially to the local church, and served on various committees. I was enrolled in the Lutheran Parochial School in which we studied religion on a regular basis. I received perfect attendance pins for 13 of my years of Sunday School participation. I can look back on my story book childhood and see the hand of God. God was drawing me and calling me from my youth, and I have vivid recollections of special moments when God was tangibly present in our local church.

For all of this I, like the Jewish Saul of Tarsus, was a complete and total heathen. I did not trust in Jesus Christ, even though I would have enthusiastically agreed with the facts of the Christmas story, and the Easter story, etc. and would have stated without hesitation that I believed in and even loved the Lord.

I am so glad that there were two meaningful encounters in my late teen years with people my age who were willing to tell me their story, and to assure me that Jesus Christ wanted to be my Lord. All I had to do, they told me, was to ask Jesus to forgive me, and to invite him to come into my life and be my personal savior. This was a rather shallow presentation of the biblical narrative, but the Spirit of God who was empowering their witness inscribed the important truths on the fleshly tables of my heart.

Paul remained in Ephesus for about two years, and continued to encourage these new disciples of Jesus.

Chapter 24

The Essence of the Gospel

---

1 Corinthians 15:1 Moreover, brethren, <u>I declare unto you the gospel</u> which I preached unto you, which also ye have received, and wherein ye stand;

2 <u>By which also ye are saved</u>, if ye keep in memory what I preached unto you, unless ye have believed in vain.

3 For I delivered unto you first of all that which I also received, how that <u>Christ died for our sins according to the scriptures</u>;

4 And that <u>he was buried</u>, and that <u>he rose again the third day according to the scriptures</u>:

5 And that he was seen of Cephas, then of the twelve:

8 And last of all he was seen of me also, as of one born out of due time.

This entire book has been about the Gospel. I have consistently asserted my conviction that the purest synopsis of the Gospel is found in 1 Corinthians 15, and that the balance of the scripture is in perfect harmony with this summary.

The Cross of Calvary is the centerpiece of the entire biblical narrative, and the rest of the Word of God either looks forward to the Cross, or back to the Cross. The Death, Burial, and Resurrection of Jesus Christ are the three strands in the Three-Fold Cord. These three strands surface throughout the Bible as the Blood, Water, and Spirit of the Old Testament prophecy, and as repentance, water baptism, and spirit baptism of the New Testament's world evangelism campaign.

There is another passage in the Bible that presents us with a synopsis of the basic fundamentals of the doctrine of Jesus Christ.

Hebrews 6:1 Therefore leaving the principles of the doctrine of Christ, let us go on unto perfection; not laying again the foundation...

The Amplified Bible says it this way:

Hebrews 6:1 Therefore let us go on and get past the elementary stage in the teachings and doctrine of Christ (the Messiah), advancing steadily toward the completeness and perfection that belong to spiritual maturity. Let us not again be laying the foundation...

The theme of this verse is that the church ought to grow up unto maturity, and stop laying the foundation over and over. In the process, the writer articulates just exactly what are the foundational first principles.

Hebrews 6:1 ...not laying again the foundation of repentance from dead works, and of faith toward God,

2 Of the doctrine of baptisms, and of laying on of hands, and of resurrection of the dead, and of eternal judgment.

3 And this will we do, if God permit.

The author of this epistle to the Hebrews writes in the hope that his readers will be able to plant their feet on solid ground and stop vacillating. He goes on to say that that it is impossible to be born again, again. There are many zealous believers who make a commitment to Jesus one day (i.e. they get "saved") only to fall back into sin the next day. On the following Sunday they are in church again going through the motions one more time. I have heard a few individuals testify that they have gotten "saved" on three different occasions, and that they are trying to stay saved this time. This is pure folly, and betrays a basic lack of understanding. The writer to the Hebrews makes this point:

Hebrews 6:4 For it is impossible for those who were once enlightened, and have tasted of the heavenly gift, and were made partakers of the Holy Ghost,

5 And have tasted the good Word of God, and the powers of the world to come,

6 If they shall fall away, to renew them again unto repentance; seeing they crucify to themselves the Son of God afresh, and put him to an open shame.

This verse is saying, most emphatically, that if a person is truly converted by the power of the Holy Ghost, it is not possible that that person can be "renewed again" or "made new, again" or "born again, again." This does not mean, as some might say, that if a Christian sins they can never be saved. It only means that if a believer sins, they do not need to get saved again. They do need to confess their sins and be reconciled to God. It seems that the Hebrew believers to whom this epistle was written were under the impression that they had to keep laying the foundation again and again. To repeat the process of repentance, water baptism, and spirit baptism again and again would constitute a real crucifying of the Son of God again and again, and would be a corruption of the pure intention of the Gospel. A similar principle was stated elsewhere in the epistle to the Hebrews.

Hebrews 10:1 For the law having a shadow of good things to come, and not the very image of the things, can never with those sacrifices which they offered year by year continually make the comers thereunto perfect.

2 For then would they not have ceased to be offered? because that the worshippers once purged should have had no more conscience of sins.

3 But in those sacrifices there is a remembrance again made of sins every year.

The writer's point here is that the temple ritual of slaughtering the sacrificial lamb again and again did not have the ultimate power to save. The true Lamb of God is only offered up once.

Hebrews 10:12 But this man, after he had offered

one sacrifice for sins for ever, sat down on the right hand of God;

13 From henceforth expecting till his enemies be made his footstool.

14 For by one offering he hath perfected for ever them that are sanctified.

By one offering he has perfected for ever them that are sanctified.

The finished work of Jesus Christ cannot be improved upon by ritual, or by repetition, or by sheer force of effort. The salvation plan of God is complete and perfect, and the Son of God himself is both the foundation and the capstone of perfection.

Hebrews Chapter 6 captures the essence of the saving work of Jesus Christ, manifested openly in the lives of ordinary believers and extended forward into eternity. We find that this list of principles perfectly harmonizes with the rest of the Holy Scriptures. The foundational principles are, in order:

- o   Repentance from Dead Works
- o   Faith toward God
- o   Baptisms (Water and Spirit)
- o   Laying on Hands (confirmation and healing)
- o   Resurrection of the Dead
- o   Eternal Judgment

Once again, the scripture presents the same salvation plan that we have chronicled throughout the Bible. There is absolutely no question that the perfect will of God for the salvation of sinners through Jesus Christ has been revealed in a three-fold fashion. These three-fold principles are more than just the starting place for people who want to be saved. They speak to us of the finished work of Jesus on the Cross, and as such are the tokens of the fulfillment of the plan of God.

Hebrews 10:14 For by one offering he hath perfected for ever them that are sanctified.

Blood, and Water, and Spirit

Death, Burial, and Resurrection

Repentance, Water Baptism, and Spirit Baptism

This is the Gospel of Jesus Christ.

Chapter 25

Conclusion

This is a book about the Gospel, and as such directly deals with the subject of world evangelism and the life or death of multiplied millions of souls. A visit to any Christian book store makes it obvious that there is a certain tension between competing ideas about how sinners can approach God, or how God saves sinners. But this confusion exists only in the minds of men and in the industries that seek to influence men's minds: Religion, Education, and Publishing. There is no confusion in God's mind, and I would suggest there is no confusion in God's word. I have tried my best in these pages to show that a consistent message of hope and salvation has been presented to the world from the very beginning and that the Lord's passion for the deliverance of sinners and the forging of a nation of overcomers has not waivered. In fact, I would say that the plan of God is right on track. There is nothing that faithless and disobedient men can do that will delay a program that is promoted by a sovereign and almighty God. And yet there are warnings in the book that we ought to carefully consider. Here are just a couple of such warnings:

Ezekiel 3:18 When I say unto the wicked, Thou shalt

surely die; and thou givest him not warning, nor speakest to warn the wicked from his wicked way, to save his life; the same wicked man shall die in his iniquity; but his blood will I require at thine hand.

This verse is a solemn warning to all who presume to show others the way of life. It was Adam who received the original admonition *"Thou shalt surely die"* and every man, woman or child who has been born since has inherited the same fate. And the same vile deceiver who set the trap for Adam has mounted a relentless misinformation and disinformation campaign that is designed for one thing: to so obscure and confuse the preaching of the Gospel that generation after generation will die in their sin.

Revelation 22:17 And the Spirit and the bride say, Come. And let him that heareth say, Come. And let him that is athirst come. And whosoever will, let him take the water of life freely.

18 For I testify unto every man that heareth the words of the prophecy of this book, If any man shall add unto these things, God shall add unto him the plagues that are written in this book:

19 And if any man shall take away from the words of the book of this prophecy, God shall take away his part out of the book of life...

Who is on the Lord's side in this epic battle? First, God himself is committed to the salvation of a remnant, and he is continually beckoning to us to come. By the Holy Spirit the hearts of men are drawn to the light like moths are drawn to a flame. Second, the Bride of Christ, which is the Church, is calling sinners to come to a God who will have mercy. This is the mission of every saint who has

A Three-Fold Cord

both heard the Gospel and received the free gift of salvation by faith through grace. Unfortunately, the masses have been duped into thinking that salvation is the job of professional clergymen, who are often ill equipped to sound the alarm with clarity. Third, those who hear the call and respond from the heart echo that call to others in their generation. This echo is probably the most effective call of all, since it finds its origin in God and is able to circle the globe practically unhindered, shared one on one with "whosoever will." The Gospel spreads like wildfire in those nations where the visible church is either controlled or suppressed, while the underground church risks everything without regard for personal preservation and political correctness. The desire for financial security and/or popularity has corrupted many a preacher. The warning in the passage of scripture above is directed toward every person who adds to or takes away anything from the words of God, and is a serious warning indeed.

This book is a call to all who study or minister the Gospel to allow God's word to say what it says. Situational ethicists compel us to blend the Word of God with current social norms to produce a message that will sell, but such attempts at smoothing out the rough spots only rob the Gospel of its power. We should begin with an assumption that God knows how to save the souls of men, and then we should freely share the Gospel of Jesus Christ in the simplest, purest form possible. I have declared in the pages of this book that a Three-Fold Cord has been threaded throughout the biblical narrative, and that this fact reveals the true essence of the Gospel. If you pull the cord in Genesis, the Bible will pucker in Revelation. An unbroken thread of truth is to be found in the words of the Law, the Prophets, the Psalms, the Gospels, the Epistles, and the Revelation. When taken together in accordance with God's prescription, truth is the cure for the sin that kills. And the truth is a person, not a collection of ideas, or even good books.

I could write another dozen pages to summarize what the Bible says about the Blood, and the Water, and the Spirit. I could recite the Apostles Creed that reminds us a Savior "suffered under Pontius Pilate, was crucified, dead, and buried; He descended into hell. The third day He arose again from the dead." And I could once again challenge you to repent of your sins, be baptized in the name of Jesus, and be filled with all the power and glory that is the down payment on your rightful inheritance. But those pages have already been written. You can read this book again, and I hope you will. I also hope that you will share what you have learned from this book with others. I encourage you to give a copy of this book to your Pastor. And finally, I would urge you to trust in the Lord Jesus Christ, and in no other. Our sovereign God is well able to accomplish his perfect will, and though he does not need my help, it will be a privilege if I find in eternity that this effort was able to aid you as you press toward the mark, for the prize of the high calling of God in Christ Jesus.

Firmly Rooted Information
A Three-Fold Cord Study Guide

The study guide version of this book - Useful as a self-study or group-study guide, each chapter is accompanied by a worksheet for personal devotions and reflection. This 6X9 Workbook can also be used by Instructors who are leading a group Bible study.

A Three-Fold Cord Supplemental Material

- **Power Point Slides** – Interactive slideshow for use by Instructors and Bible Teachers.

- **Student Handouts** – Can be passed out to Bible study participants for pre-requisite study or as homework assignments.

- **Bible Reference Chart** – Color chart that organizes all Bible verses for a study on A Three-Fold Cord. Can be provided to all Bible study participants. The chart supports and encourages independent self-study. 8½ X 14.

- **Quad-Fold Gospel Tract** – Shares the message of the Blood, the Water and the Spirit in a tract format. The Bible Reference Chart is duplicated on the reverse side.

CPSIA information can be obtained
at www.ICGtesting.com
Printed in the USA
LVHW08s0950060818
586106LV00001B/2/P

9 781456 727963